MRT

PRINCETON STUDIES IN INTERNATIONAL FINANCE

No. 79, December 1995

INTERNATION~~~~~~~~~~~~~~ PRICES, MACROECONOMIC PERFORMANCE, AND POLITICS IN SUB-SAHARAN AFRICA

ANGUS S. DEATON

AND

RONALD I. MILLER

INTERNATIONAL FINANCE SECTION

DEPARTMENT OF ECONOMICS
PRINCETON UNIVERSITY
PRINCETON, NEW JERSEY

HF
1040.9
.A357
D43
1995

INTERNATIONAL FINANCE SECTION
EDITORIAL STAFF

Library of Congress Cataloging-in-Publication Data

C

Deaton, Angus S.
    International commodity prices, macroeconomic performance, and politics in Sub-Saharan Africa / Angus S. Deaton and Ronald I. Miller.
    p. cm. — (Princeton studies in international finance, ISSN 0081-8070 ; no. 79)
    Includes bibliographical references.
    ISBN 0-88165-251-2 (pbk.) : $11.00
    1. Primary commodities—Prices—Africa, Sub-Saharan. 2. Africa, Sub-Saharan—Economic conditions. 3. Africa, Sub-Saharan—Politics and government. I. Ronald I. Miller, 1966– . II. Title. III. Series
HF1040.9.A357D43 1995
338.5′2′0967—dc20
                                        95-25494
                                              CIP

Printed in the United States of America by Princeton University Printing Services at Princeton, New Jersey

International Standard Serial Number: 0081-8070

CONTENTS

FIGURES

TABLES

1 INTRODUCTION

The exports of many Sub-Saharan African countries are concentrated in a relatively small number of primary commodities, commodities for which world prices are volatile and values of which have dropped to historically low levels in recent years. Fluctuations in commodity prices induce fluctuations in real national incomes and pose problems for macroeconomic management. These problems are often badly handled,[1] and several observers implicate the commodity-price booms of the 1970s in the debt crises of the 1980s (Krueger, 1987; Greene, 1989; Sachs, 1988). Sachs, for example, notes that when commodity prices are rising more rapidly than the rate of interest on international loans, countries can service debt through fresh borrowing while simultaneously reducing the ratio of debt to exports. In the 1970s, this opportunity was seized by several developing countries that had previously had little or no access to private international capital markets. When the boom in commodity prices came to an end, some of these borrowers found themselves unable to service their accumulated debt.

Other authors argue that booms in government revenue lead to hastily executed investment programs that involve low-return and irreversible projects or to good but overambitious projects that are abandoned when revenue falls. Hirschman (1977) cites, as an early example, the mid-nineteenth-century Peruvian guano boom, the benefits of which were squandered in railway investments, and Collier and

Earlier versions of the results reported in this study were reported in Deaton (1993a, 1993b) and Deaton and Miller (1993). For comments on the earlier papers, we thank Robert Bates, Tim Besley, Henry Bienen, Anne Case, Paul Collier, John Cuddington, Ron Duncan, Jeffrey Herbst, Stanley Fischer, Jim Fox, Albert Hirschman, Yoon Joo Lee, John Londregan, Christina Paxson, John Waterbury, and participants in the African Economic Research Consortium meeting in Nairobi in May 1995. Henry Bienen, Anne Case, Ron Duncan, John Londregan, and Guy Whitten helped provide data, and Alex Michaelides, Tara Mukerjee, and Yajai Yodin provided research assistance. The work reported here was partly funded under a cooperative agreement between the Institute for Policy Reform and the United States Agency for International Development (USAID), Co-operative Agreement No. PDC-0095-A-00-1126-00, and partly by the National Science Foundation under grant number SES-9223668.

[1] See Tanzi, 1986; Balassa, 1988; Gelb, 1988; Bevan, Collier, and Gunning, 1989, 1990; Cuddington, 1989; Gavin, 1993; Little et al., 1993.

Gunning (1994) attribute the Egyptian loss of the Suez Canal to the unsustainable Egyptian public-expenditure programs following the cotton-price boom during the U.S. Civil War.

One of the most thoroughly examined recent commodity-price episodes is the 1976–79 Kenyan coffee-price boom explored by Bevan, Collier, and Gunning (1989, 1990, 1991). Using the methods applied in that investigation, the authors have led a team of researchers looking at a series of other commodity-price shocks in twenty-three countries in Africa, Asia, and Latin America. In an early overview of their work (1991), they conclude that certain aspects of the Kenyan boom generalize, although there are considerable differences across countries. They argue that (1) even though governments initially try to save windfalls, they finally invest far in excess of their saving, so that the final legacy of the windfall is debt, (2) such investments are usually of poor quality and have low returns, (3) governments raise their current expenditures in a way that is difficult to reverse when the boom turns to slump and that they thus destabilize the economy when sharp and often harmful cuts have finally to be made, (4) governments do not make appropriate use of international capital markets, and (5) the results depend little on whether the windfall income from the boom accrues in the first instance to the government or to the private sector. This is so because tax revenue automatically increases as private income increases and because the government makes discretionary increases in tax rates in order to capture a larger share of the boom (for example, new taxes on windfall profits).

This study looks at the experience of Sub-Saharan Africa in dealing with commodity-price variability and discusses whether poor macroeconomic results should be attributed to the inherent difficulty of predicting commodity-price fluctuations or, rather, to flawed internal political and fiscal arrangements. In an attempt to establish the facts and to cast light on some of the mechanisms, it examines pan-African econometric evidence on the effects of commodity-price fluctuations on national output and its components. It also addresses the effects of commodity prices on political outcomes and asks whether the survival of African leaders is affected by the changes in national output associated with fluctuations in international prices. The emphasis on econometric evidence is different from the less formal approach of the studies reported in Collier et al. (1995), but the two approaches are more complementary than competitive. Indeed, the conclusions reached in this study are not very different from those in the final overview paper by Collier and Gunning (1995).

2

Table 1 presents growth rates of export prices for twelve African countries from 1980 to 1990, together with two measures of their coefficient of variation. From 1975 to 1980, all of these countries benefited from export-price growth, an experience that was reversed in the following quinquennium. From 1980 to 1990, Nigeria and Ghana, two economies usually thought to have performed poorly, experienced large fluctuations in export prices according to both the measures shown. Zaire and Zambia, both largely dependent on copper, also experienced high variability. The experience of Tanzania, which experienced low variability, demonstrates only that the absence of commodity-price fluctuations is no guarantee of success.

Much of the variation in unit values can be explained by movements in the world prices of the underlying commodities. Figures 1 and 2 show historical data on the nominal U.S. dollar prices for cocoa, coffee, copper, and cotton, four commodities that are important in Sub-Saharan Africa. Two are "tree" crops, one a metal, and one an annual crop. (Cocoa and coffee are important for two of the countries, Ghana and Kenya, on whose experience we draw below.) The U.S. consumer price index (CPI) is superimposed on each of the graphs to give some idea of long-term changes in real purchasing power—both internationally and, if purchasing-power parity (PPP) holds in the long term, domestically. These graphs have features that are characteristic of many primary commodity prices relevant to developing countries. They show extended periods when the price is relatively stable, punctuated by shorter periods of extreme volatility when prices flare upward in peaks that typically last several years. With the possible exception of cotton in August 1986, there are no downward spikes from periods of quiescence. Volatility has usually been greater since 1970, although some of the increase reflects the largely mechanical effect of denominating the price in a single currency during an age of fluctuating exchange rates. (If primary-commodity prices are affected by the aggregate demand of the industrial countries, fluctuations in the value of the dollar relative to a basket of other country currencies will cause fluctuations in the dollar price of commodities even when the price is constant in terms of all the currencies together.) Although nominal prices exhibit upward trends, they are typically insufficient even to match inflation, so that real prices have been constant or falling. The CPI has increased about fivefold since the mid-1950s. By contrast, a pound of cocoa or coffee fetched the same price in nominal dollars in the early 1990s as it did in 1955, although copper and cotton prices approximately tripled. The presence of a long-term downward trend in the real prices of primary

3

TABLE 1

Price Growth and Variability in Twelve African Countries

	Growth Rates			Coefficient of Variation		Main Commodity Exports
	1975–80	1980–85	1985–90	(1)	(2)	
Cameroon	15.2	-2.9	-6.7	18.8	21.5	Cocoa, coffee, cotton, oil
Ivory Coast	15.6	-3.0	-4.4	10.8	22.2	Cocoa, coffee. cotton, logs, palm, sugar
Ghana	15.4	-4.0	-8.5	15.0	17.6	Bauxite, cocoa, gold, logs, manganese
Kenya	13.7	-3.4	-4.2	12.0	18.0	Coffee, sisal, tea
Madagascar	13.2	-1.2	-0.4	6.7	18.7	Coffee, sisal, sugar
Nigeria	20.2	-4.0	-3.8	31.2	25.8	Cocoa, oil
Senegal	6.7	-3.6	4.5	9.5	14.9	Groundnut oil, phosphates
Sudan	10.1	-6.2	5.3	12.4	12.0	Cotton, groundnuts
Tanzania	11.4	-3.8	0.1	5.9	8.3	Coffee, cotton, sisal, sugar, tea, tobacco
Zaire	11.0	-5.6	4.5	13.2	16.9	Coffee, copper, gold, oil, logs
Zambia	10.9	-8.1	12.4	28.5	28.2	Copper
Zimbabwe	9.6	-5.4	7.3	14.4	9.3	Cotton, gold, meat, nickel, sugar, tea, tobacco

NOTE: Columns 1, 2, and 3 are calculated from the merchandise export-price series in the World Bank's 1994 *World Data CD-ROM*. Column 4 is the coefficient of variation from 1980 to 1990 of the unit values. Column 5 is the coefficient of variation from 1980 to 1990 of the real-commodity-price series described in Chapter 4. The second estimate differs from the first in being real and probably more reliable, although it covers only a selection of major exports.

FIGURE 1

COCOA AND COFFEE PRICES

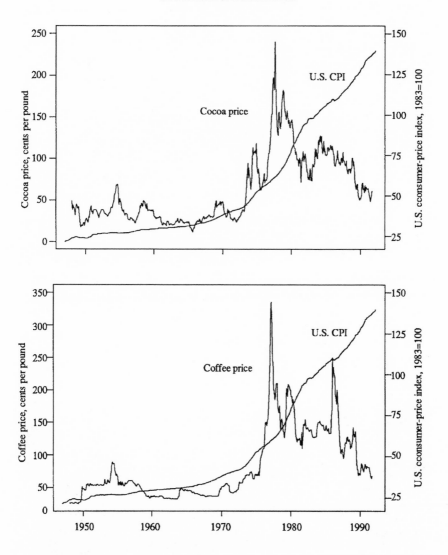

NOTE: Until September 1977, the cocoa price is mid-month in Accra (IMF); from October 1977 to October 1980, it is the average monthly price in Accra (WB); from November 1980, it is the mid-month price in Ivory Coast (CRB). Coffee prices are mid-month Brazilian prices (CRB).
SOURCES: IMF, *International Financial Statistics* (1994), World Bank Commodity Division (WB); Commodity Research Bureau (CRB), *CRB Infotech Commodity Data* (1992).

FIGURE 2

COPPER AND COTTON PRICES

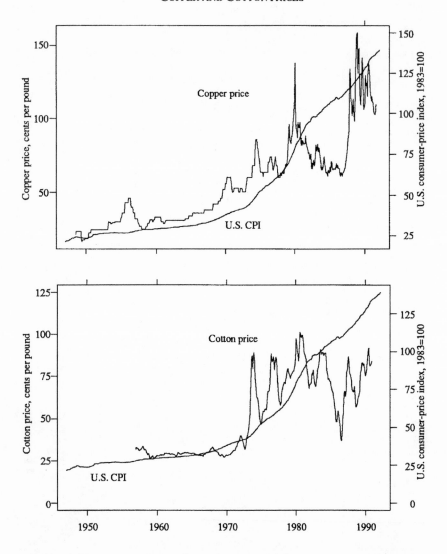

NOTE: Copper prices are mid-month for electrolytic copper, Connecticut Valley (CRB), and cotton prices are monthly averages of U.S. medium staple (IMF).

SOURCES: IMF, *International Financial Statistics* (1994) and Commodity Research Bureau (CRB) *CRB Infotech Commodity Data* (1992).

commodities in general—the Prebisch-Singer hypothesis—has been much investigated and remains controversial; variability is large relative to trend, and the results can be sensitive to the period investigated. Prices in the early 1990s are low by any standard, and recent investigations tend to find downward trends (Grilli and Yang, 1988; Cuddington and Urzúa, 1989; Cuddington, 1992; Ardeni and Wright, 1992; Cuddington and Feyzioglu, 1993).

Although we shall have something further to say about trends, the focus in this study is on variability and the associated stabilization problems. Chapter 2 discusses the design of stabilization policy and what a government needs to know about commodity prices, assuming that stabilization and growth are its goals. If reliable forecasts of future prices are available, booms and slumps can be treated for what they are and policy set accordingly. Less precise information is also useful, and an understanding of the general nature of specific commodity prices, though not predicting the precise dates on which booms will start or end, can indicate the average length of booms and slumps and can be used to calculate the costs and benefits of the various possible stabilization policies.

Much of the criticism of African policy has been made with the benefit of hindsight; it is a good deal easier to forecast prices once the future is safely past. In reality, there is much uncertainty, and commodity prices are very hard to forecast. Structural models that incorporate a great deal of specific and detailed information about supply and demand have been used in the past, but their track record in forecasting prices has been very mixed. Although they successfully predicted the ends of the cocoa and coffee booms of the mid-1970s, they have not otherwise provided forecasts that would have aided stabilization. Nonstructural time-series methods are even less successful; indeed, as we shall see, the behavior of commodity prices could hardly be better designed to frustrate the standard methods that, routinely applied, lead to clearly absurd recommendations. Although the econometric analysis is not a success, its very failure tells us a good deal about which kinds of policies are sensible and which are not. We argue that stabilization rules based on a notion of permanent income, such as international compensation or sterilization schemes, are neither desirable nor likely to be feasible.

The difficulty of forecasting commodity prices is not the only constraint on policy in Africa. Chapter 3 looks at the economics and political economy of taxation and government expenditure in the context of African countries exporting primary commodities and discusses

7

arguments that African fiscal and political arrangements compromise the ability to react to external shocks. Although the discussion is largely a review, it suggests a number of hypotheses that can be examined empirically. We turn to these in Chapters 4 and 5, where we use pooled time-series cross-sectional data from thirty-two Sub-Saharan African countries to examine the dynamic effects of commodity-price changes on national output and its components. Chapter 4 explains the procedures used and provides baseline results together with an examination of their robustness to different data choices (an important matter when dealing with the uncertainties of African statistics). Chapter 5 extends the baseline model to examine a number of other issues: asymmetric responses between booms and slumps, differences between booms in mineral and nonmineral prices, the effects of agricultural tax regimes on the ways in which commodity-price shocks affect the economy, the effects of international commodity-price changes on domestic inflation, and the effects of commodity-price fluctuations on the accumulation of debt. The experience of individual countries is also considered, to try to match the pan-African "typical" results with those from the country studies.

Although some of the findings are consistent with the typically negative tone in much of the literature, most are not. The evidence hardly supports the notion that African policymakers handle commodity-price fluctuations well, but it suggests that the effects of price increases have been generally benevolent, as might at first be supposed. Increases in prices are associated most strongly with increased investment and, subsequently, with increased consumption and output. As is to be expected, there are short-term negative effects on the real balance of trade, but there is no evidence of a medium- or long-term deterioration associated with a commodity-price boom. Our examination of the individual country evidence confirms the heterogeneity of experience, although there is clear evidence overall that the economies of African countries grow faster when the prices of their exports are increasing than they do when prices are falling. Indeed, the estimates suggest that about one-fifth of the decline in the rate of economic growth in Africa during 1980–85 as compared with 1970–75 can be attributed to the behavior of international commodity prices. And although it is true that the countries that experienced commodity-price booms in the late 1970s accumulated a large amount of long-term external debt then and in the 1980s, so did many other African countries that experienced no such booms or for which commodity prices were actually declining; we find no clear association between debt and commodity-price booms.

In line with the predictions of both Dutch-disease and construction-boom models that domestic prices—or, more precisely, the prices of nontradables—should rise in response to a commodity-price boom, there is evidence that commodity-price increases generate inflation. The effect is modest, however, particularly once we have eliminated the mechanical accounting effects of commodity prices on the price measures. The tests of robustness, using different data and different methodologies, generate results that are different in detail, and the timing of the effects of international prices is sensitive to the use of "official" versus "purchasing-power-parity" national-accounting data. The broad picture is the same, however; increases in the world prices of commodity exports are beneficial to African economies, and decreases are harmful. We find some evidence that fluctuations in mineral prices, including oil prices, have less effect on African economies than have fluctuations in the prices of other, largely agricultural, commodities. We find no marked difference between countries with regard to stabilization success that corresponds to differences in the way commodity exports are taxed, and we find no strong evidence of asymmetry in the effects of commodity-price booms and slumps.

Our results support the conclusions in Bevan, Collier, and Gunning (1991) on the diversity of experience across different African countries, but unlike their work and more in accord with the results of Collier and Gunning (1995), our study finds no strong evidence for the general applicability of what has become the conventional wisdom, that commodity booms are generally harmful. The heterogeneity is not surprising, given the large differences in political and economic institutions across Africa, not to mention the differences in the commodities themselves and in their conditions of production, marketing, and taxation. It is therefore naive to expect the econometric analysis of many countries together to reveal more than the broadest generalities. Nevertheless, we believe that if the conventional wisdom is to be useful as a generality— as opposed to simply describing events in a few countries—it should be consistent with the econometric evidence.

If the case study and econometric results are ultimately different, which should we believe? Each methodology has its strengths and weaknesses. The case studies, and particularly those of the Kenyan coffee boom, contain a wealth of detailed local information that can never be brought into the econometric methods. It is possible, with this detail, to study one country at a time and to look for both similarities and differences between countries. This is much more difficult for the econometric time-series methods, because individual country series

9

are relatively short and pooling across countries is required for statistical precision. There are compensating difficulties with the case studies, however. Some of these are general to the method, and some are specific to the methodology used originally by Bevan, Collier, and Gunning for Kenya and applied by their collaborators to an additional twenty-two countries. All of the studies are concerned with specific price episodes and, although not excluding other periods, give the greatest attention to the events surrounding the period selected. Such selections are not always obvious or uncontroversial. They face exactly the same difficulties that have plagued the dating of business cycles in macroeconomics, where such methods have been supplanted by time-series methods that do not require prior identification of booms and slumps. For example, in Aron's (1992) insightful study of Zambia, there was a copper-price "boom" from 1964 to 1974, followed by a series of negative shocks. But the copper price fell almost continuously from 1970, and it is not clear why the drop should not be treated as a single decline, rather than as split into two parts, that is, the end of a boom followed by the beginning of a slump. Similar timing issues arise for other booms in other countries.

One of the key underlying issues is the treatment of expectations, and in this regard, it is very hard to see any real alternative to time-series analysis. Bevan, Collier, and Gunning draw a distinction between "inclusive" and "exclusive" expectations, the latter describing those cases in which price events are not only unexpected, but are so unexpected as to contradict the previous expectation *mechanisms*. Structural breaks in stochastic processes are potentially important phenomena and are not well handled by time-series methods. However, the distinction between "inclusive" and "exclusive" expectations is perhaps even harder to manage in practice than are structural breaks in econometrics. The stochastic processes that describe commodity prices are very poorly understood in any case, and even official forecasts—such as those of the World Bank—have often been weak. It is thus clearly impossible to tell whether a discrepancy between an expectation and outcome is the result of routine forecast error, of structural change, or simply of poor (or politically biased) forecasting. We would argue for a neutral approach to such matters, confining our attention to the observable impacts of prices and avoiding insupportable distinctions about expectations.

The heart of the problem is the isolation of the effects of commodity prices from what would otherwise have happened. Bevan, Collier, and Gunning construct explicit counterfactuals, predicting the state of the economy without the commodity-price shock. Although they can bring to bear a variety of data sources and information to this task, this is surely an area in which econometric analysis has an overwhelming advantage. Like econometric analysis, the counterfactual case studies use past data and past relationships, but they are nearly always based on simple extrapolation of ratios from the years immediately prior to the event. It is hard to think of cases in which the automatic controls in a vector autoregression (VAR) would not do this better. Our view is that the appropriate general methodology is to use case studies as a vehicle for generating hypotheses. Without the material from country studies, by economists and political scientists as well as by development practitioners in the field, we would have little knowledge of the causes and consequences of policymaking in Africa. The role of the econometric evidence, however, which in the African context is at its best when data from many countries can be pooled, is to test the validity of the generalizations. If the country-study results do indeed reveal general laws, these laws should be apparent in the formal analysis. If they are not—and they do not seem to be for the conventional wisdom on commodity prices—the country studies remain country studies and should not be seen as more than that.

Chapter 6 returns to the relation between politics and prices but examines the reverse causation, from prices to politics. The literatures in both economics and political science have demonstrated a link between economic growth and the survival of political leaders, although the direction of causation has remained unclear. Successful economic performance may enhance the probability of political survival, but it is also possible that growth in national output reflects political stability, or more precisely (because it is far from being the same), the absence of changes in leadership. World commodity prices are set in international markets that, with a few exceptions, are not influenced by the political events in a single country. The results of Chapters 4 and 5 demonstrate that fluctuations in the international prices of commodities affect the growth of national output. As a result, it is possible to sort out the causality between growth and leader survival using the behavior of commodity prices. If the causality runs from economic growth to political change, commodity prices should be correlated with political change, a correlation that has no reason to be present if economic growth is the result of a stable political environment. Although the results are clouded by statistical uncertainty, the balance of the evidence leans toward the interpretation that economics are driving politics, not the other way around.

11

2 STABILIZATION AND COMMODITY PRICES

Understanding and Predicting Prices

An appropriate response to commodity-price shocks requires that some judgment be made about the implications of those shocks for the future. A choice between stabilization and adjustment requires that shocks be decomposed into permanent and transitory components, something that cannot be done without a model of the process. In some cases, the reason for a price change is evident, and that reason can tell us how long the change is likely to persist. A frost that destroys a single crop has different consequences than a disease that destroys an orchard of trees. More generally, there is a great deal of information about specific commodity markets, and this can be incorporated into structural econometric models, most notably by the World Bank, which issues regular forecasts for more than thirty commodities. An alternative approach is to apply the methods of time-series analysis and to use the history of prices to develop a model of price behavior. We start with this second approach, following through a more or less standard time-series analysis for the four commodity prices illustrated in the figures. For more thoroughgoing analyses in the same spirit, see Cuddington and Urzúa (1989), Gersovitz and Paxson (1990), and Cuddington (1992).

Time-Series Analysis

Suppose, for example, that we wish to forecast the cocoa-price series shown in Figure 1. If we use the average monthly data, combining the data from the International Monetary Fund's (IMF) *International Financial Statistics* (1994) and the Commodity Research Bureau's *CRB Infotech Commodity Data* (1992), we have 525 observations from January 1948 to September 1991, a sample that would seem large enough to obtain a precise characterization of the process. To avoid time aggregation, it would be better to use mid-month or end-month prices, but such data are not always available for long-enough time spans.

Although there are a number of ways to proceed, one obvious way is to deflate by a price index—in this case, the U.S. CPI—and to take logarithms. The resulting series might then be modeled as a linear autoregressive process, with the large number of lags permitted by the long time period. Such a regression gives the following results, with

12

absolute *t*-values in parentheses:

$$\ln p_t = -0.00039 + 1.167 \ln p_{t-1} - 0.127 \ln p_{t-2} + \dots, \qquad (1)$$
$$ (0.1) \qquad (24.1) \qquad (1.7)$$

where there are an additional forty-six lags (making four years in total) that are not shown but that typically have small coefficients (the smallest being –0.06 and the largest 0.11) and standard errors that are about 0.07. The equation has an R^2 statistic of 0.975. The sum of the coefficients on the first two lags is close to unity, which suggests that the logarithm of the cocoa price has a unit root. Following standard time-series practice, therefore, we regress the growth rate of prices on lagged rates of growth. The result is, as expected given (1),

$$\Delta \ln p_t = -0.00207 + 0.1702 \Delta \ln p_{t-1} + \dots, \qquad (2)$$
$$ (0.5) \qquad (3.5)$$

where, once again, we have included but not shown the succeeding forty-seven lagged differences. This regression has an R^2 of 0.0951 (for the growth rate of prices), and if we apply the standard Dickey–Fuller test, it is impossible to reject the hypothesis of the unit root. The additional lags do not add significantly to the explanatory power of the regression. If they are excluded, the coefficient on the lagged difference rises to 0.2148 and the R^2 falls to 0.0464. Equation (2), or its counterpart with higher lags excluded, is a simple, parsimonious model of the data, and although we could go on to apply more sophisticated techniques, it represents the typical result that is obtained when standard time-series analysis is applied to commodity-price data.

Corresponding analysis for the prices of coffee, copper, and cotton gives the results shown in the top panel of Table 2. For all four commodities, it is impossible to reject the hypothesis that there is a unit root, and so, following standard practice and ignoring the typically low power of unit-root tests, we present the regressions of first differences on their lags. For cocoa and coffee, a first-order specification fits the data well, and higher lags are neither individually nor jointly significant. For copper and cotton, the data prefer second-order specifications, as is shown in the table.

Consider now the stabilization problem viewed in the light of these results. We illustrate using the first-order model for the (log) price change, as for cocoa and coffee, which is

$$\Delta \ln p_t - \mu = \beta_1 (\Delta \ln p_{t-1} - \mu) + u_t, \qquad (3)$$

where μ is the mean rate of change of the real price. From equation

13

(3), expectations satisfy

$$E_t(\Delta \ln p_{t+k} - \mu) = \beta_1^k(\Delta \ln p_t - \mu) \qquad (4)$$

for any date k periods ahead. The change in expectations from $t - 1$ to t is therefore

$$(E_t - E_{t-1})\Delta \ln p_{t+k} = \beta_1^k(E_t - E_{t-1})\Delta \ln p_t = \beta_1^k u_t . \qquad (5)$$

The change in expectations of the log price in $t + k$ is therefore

$$(E_t - E_{t-1})\ln p_{t+k} = \sum_{j=0}^{k}(E_t - E_{t-1})\Delta \ln p_{t+k} = \sum_{j=0}^{k}\beta_1^k u_t = u_t \frac{1 - \beta_1^{k+1}}{1 - \beta_1} . \qquad (6)$$

Because u_t is the current "news" in the price, this formula says that the ultimate effect of the news on prices far enough into the future is obtained by multiplying it by a factor $(1 - \beta_1)^{-1}$. A parallel calculation for the second-order autoregressive model gives the (obvious enough) result that the multiplier should be $(1 - \beta_1 - \beta_2)^{-1}$. For cocoa and coffee, the long-term multipliers are 1.28 and 1.56, respectively. For copper and cotton, the corresponding long-term multipliers are 1.27

TABLE 2

COMMODITY PRICES: TIME-SERIES ESTIMATES

	Cocoa	Coffee	Copper	Cotton
Constant	−0.0021 (0.6)	−0.0010 (0.4)	−0.0002 (0.1)	−0.0008 (0.4)
$d\ln p_{t-1}$	0.2148 (5.0)	0.3599 (8.8)	0.3666 (8.5)	0.6350 (12.9)
$d\ln p_{t-2}$	—	—	−0.1594 (3.7)	−0.1508 (3.1)
Multiplier When Following Lags Are Included				
1	1.14	1.56	1.47	2.22
1, 2	1.32	1.59	1.27	1.92
1, 2, 3	1.32	1.61	1.22	2.13
1, 2, 12–14	1.28	1.32	1.12	1.25
1, 2, 12–14, 24–26	1.16	1.27	1.01	1.04
1–48	0.88	1.32	0.77	1.22
Cuddington Multipliers				
Low-order model	0.64	0.38	1.00	0.56
High-order model	—	0.26	—	0.15
Deaton and Laroque Nonparametric Multiplier				
	0.24	0.11	0.22	0.13

NOTE: Numbers in parentheses are absolute t-values.
SOURCES: Cuddington, "Long-Run Trends in 26 Primary Commodity Prices" (1992); Deaton and Laroque, "On the Behavior of Commodity Prices" (1992).

and 1.92. These numbers tell us that unanticipated changes in prices are only a signal of more to come, and that the long-term effects of an unexpected price increase will actually be *larger* than the immediate effects—in the case of cotton, almost twice as large.

If these numbers are accepted, and if we ignore complications related to stochastic output and possible interrelations between output and price, then an unanticipated commodity boom should lead, not to saving, but to borrowing, because consumption should adjust to the newly anticipated long-term levels, which are even larger than the already inflated current price. Although some African countries seem to have followed such a strategy, elementary economics and common sense rebel against the belief that such behavior is optimal. We know that the prices of agricultural crops, such as cocoa, coffee, and cotton are affected by the weather and other natural sources of fluctuations. We also know that these sources of variation are essentially transitory. Even for tree crops, where frosts, fires, or diseases may damage enough trees to affect harvests for several years to come, it is hard to imagine that weather-induced price changes have long-term consequences for price levels. That is not to say that some component of price innovations, such as that caused by the development of synthetic substitutes or by demand-side shocks, will not have permanent effects on price. Even weather-induced price increases may persuade new suppliers to enter the market, with permanent effects on market structure and on price. But if we accept the generally held view that most of the variance in commodity prices comes from the supply side, only a small fraction of any given price innovation can possibly be permanent, so that long-term estimates of multipliers of unity are clearly incorrect.

What has gone wrong, and why does the econometric analysis, which is standard enough, lead to the wrong answer? Part of the problem (although only part) lies in the bias that is built into time-series methodology in favor of parsimonious models, especially when parsimony is interpreted as favoring low-order lags. The addition of higher lags to the models in Table 2 gives coefficients that are neither individually nor jointly statistically significant, but their presence affects the conclusions about the long-term multipliers. Consider the second panel. The first three rows show the multipliers when one, two, and three lags are included, the fourth row, when lags one, two, twelve, thirteen, and fourteen are included (to capture effects from the previous year), the fifth row, when these plus the same lags from two years before are included, and the last, when all lags up to forty-eight are included. Although the patterns are not uniform, it is clear that including more

15

lags tends to decrease the size of the eventual multiplier. In the cases of cocoa and copper with all lags included, the multipliers are less than unity, showing that at least some of the original effects of the shocks are expected to wear off. Even so, the lowest number is still 0.77, for copper, which means that three-quarters of all price innovations can be expected to persist indefinitely, something that is quite implausible given the long-term behavior of copper prices shown in Figure 2.

Both the graphical evidence and the fact that the multipliers decrease when more lags are included suggest that the problem may come from a failure of the econometric analysis to pay sufficient attention to low-frequency movements in the data. It might therefore be argued that yearly data would give better results. In fact, there exist annual data for these (and some other) commodities back to 1900, and these data give us a longer span to work with, even though there can be legitimate doubts about whether the behavior of commodity prices during and immediately after World War I (for example) is of much relevance for policymaking in developing countries today. These data have been analyzed in a number of papers.

Cuddington (1992) provides an excellent and careful time-series analysis using more sophisticated methods than the simple results above. He is also led to specifications with unit roots but fits the differences using moving-average rather than autoregressive models. He estimates "low-order" models for a wide range of commodities and higher-order specifications for a smaller number of cases for which the low-order models are deemed to be unsatisfactory. The resulting multipliers are given in the third panel of Table 2; note that these are multipliers for an *annual* innovation in log price, as opposed to a *monthly* innovation in the second panel, so that the numbers are not strictly comparable. Apart from copper, for which Cuddington estimates a random walk, so that the long-term multiplier is unity, the multipliers are now all less than one. When the higher-order models are preferred, as they are for coffee and cotton, the estimates are lower than for the low-order models, as was the case for the monthly data.

The final panel of Table 2 shows estimates from Deaton and Laroque (1992), who use the same data Cuddington uses. These are nonparametric estimates of the multiplier (see Cochrane, 1988, for the basic theory) and can be loosely regarded as what would be estimated from a regression containing an infinite number of lags. These numbers are lower still and essentially confirm the visual impression from the graphs that innovations have no long-term consequences; eventually, prices return to their usual levels. Gersovitz and Paxson (1990, appendix A) also calculate persistence measures—in their case, for annual data from 1950 to 1987. Although the results are less dramatic than for the longer-term data, the persistence measures are, once again, typically lower than would be suggested by low-order autoregressive moving-average (ARMA) models.

Clearly, time-series analysis does a very poor job of providing commodity-price models that are useful for stabilization policy. Policy advice based on standard low-order models is absurd, leading not merely to too little stabilization, but to destabilization. The analysis suggests that current fluctuations will last forever, so that anyone who believes the results will be continuously surprised by the tendency of prices to revert to long-term levels. The failure of time-series analysis to capture long-term dynamics is not specific to commodity prices. It occurs whenever series are persistent in the short term but slowly revert to either a fixed level or to a deterministic trend. For example, Cochrane (1991, p. 208), commenting on Campbell's and Perron's (1991) survey of unit roots in macroeconomics, writes:

> So long as you do not get too creative with breaking trends and structural shifts, any tests tell you that interest rates have unit roots, and lag selection procedures indicate a near random walk structure. That model does quite well for one-step-ahead forecasting. Yet, interest rates are almost certainly stationary in levels.

Although it is clearly possible to use more sophisticated time-series models to yield more sensible results—and the work by Cuddington and Feyzioglu (1993) on long-memory processes is an example—there are obvious dangers in trying to build time-series models without attention to the economic processes that generate commodity prices.

Structural Models of Commodity Prices

Time-series analysis makes no use of a great deal of commodity–market information that would seem to be relevant for predicting the future. There have been changes in the techniques of production for many commodities, and the development of synthetic and other substitutes has led to changes on the demand side. New countries have become producers, and new markets have been developed for consumption. In the shorter term, the vintages of tree crop orchards are observable, and the information can be used to project production several years into the future; cocoa trees, for example, produce no yield until they are four years old. All this information can be incorporated into forecasts if detailed structural models are constructed. Such work is carried out by

17

a number of market consultants, most conspicuously by the World Bank, the forecasts of which are widely noted by both market analysts and country governments.

The World Bank has little choice but to construct such models, not only because it requires unconditional forecasts—for project evaluation, for example—but also because it needs to be able to assess the effects on price of market developments and deliberate policies—for example, the World Bank's encouragement to several countries to expand their cocoa production simultaneously. These models tend to follow a common structure, with detailed modeling of supply and demand, typically by major producers and consumers or at least by region, together with some treatment of stockholding and price determined so as to clear markets. For example, Akiyama and Duncan (1982) include, in their analysis of the world coffee market, separate demand equations for the United States, the European Economic Community, the Middle East, Scandinavia, Southern Europe, the centrally planned economies, Japan, other industrial countries, Brazil, and the rest of the world, and separate supply equations for Brazil (with distinct equations for tree stocks and production), Colombia, El Salvador, Guatemala, Indonesia, Ivory Coast, and the rest of the world. They complete their model with equations for the demand for inventories by consumers, by the United States, and by producers.

Past forecasts of price trends have been most kindly supplied to us by Ron Duncan of the International Trade Division of the World Bank, and some of these are shown for the four illustrative commodities in Figures 3 and 4. In each case, the solid line is the annual average actual nominal price; the units are the same as in Figures 1 and 2, but the averaging makes the graphs less variable. The broken lines show the Bank's various nominal-price forecasts and in each case are shown as beginning from the actual price in the year in which the forecast was made. This is somewhat misleading, because the forecasts are often made early in the year (the 1980 forecast was issued in January), so that the forecasters do not have the benefit of the actual price in the year in which the forecast is made.

It is not our purpose here to assess either the usefulness of structural forecasts in general or of the World Bank's forecasts in particular. Rather, we are concerned with the consequences for policy of these estimates being used by African policymakers for stabilization purposes, and whether these forecasts, which are made by a thoroughly professional and well-informed group, are more useful than are the results from the time-series models.

18

FIGURE 3

COCOA AND COFFEE PRICES: ACTUALS AND FORECASTS

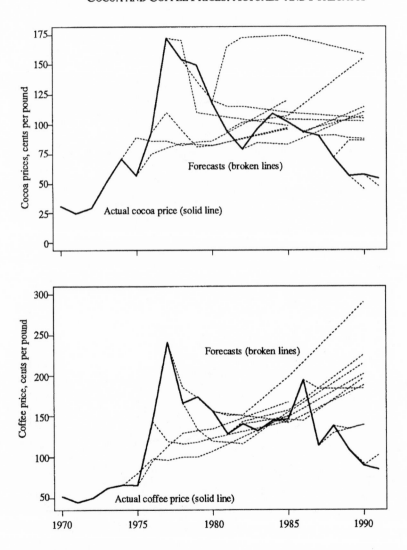

SOURCE: World Bank Commodity Division.

FIGURE 4

COPPER AND COTTON PRICES: ACTUALS AND FORECASTS

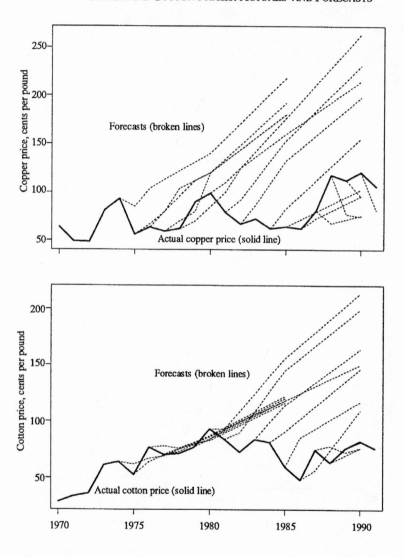

SOURCE: World Bank Commodity Division.

It certainly makes a difference. For cocoa, the World Bank models did not predict the boom from 1976 to 1982, even when it was under way; once the peak was reached, however, the forecasts of its demise over the next five to eight years were accurate. Even before the boom, in 1974 and 1975, the ten-year-ahead forecasts were correct. Subsequent to the boom, in 1980 and 1981, the Bank was forecasting another resurgence in price, a resurgence that did not materialize. If stabilization policy, say in Ghana or Ivory Coast, had been based on these predictions, it would have been conservative during the 1976–80 boom, which would certainly have been more sensible than what actually happened, or what would have happened had spending been increased by more than the price increases (as would be implied by blindly following the [low-order] time-series results). Subsequent experience with the forecasts would not have been so favorable; if the numbers had been treated seriously, they could have prolonged the attempts to stabilize the apparently temporary fall in prices and postponed the adjustment that was eventually necessary in any case. Even so, it is hard to imagine almost any combination of circumstances that would have allowed Ghana or Ivory Coast to borrow enough to sustain consumption at the levels of the early 1980s. When prices are declining, the time-series models will tend to overstate the consequences for the future and thus lead to spending cuts that are too extreme and to overadjustment downward. In the event, both Ghana and Ivory Coast were forced into adjustment programs, so that given the reality of international capital markets, it hardly matters whether the recent downswing was seen as permanent or cyclical. Either way, consumption would have had to be adjusted down.

The story for coffee is similar to that for cocoa, with the boom only slowly recognized but its demise correctly predicted. Once again, however, there was a marked degree of false optimism after the boom, so that until 1987, the World Bank was forecasting prices for 1990 that were several times higher than the subsequent real levels proved to be. The putative effects on stabilization policy are therefore much the same as for cocoa. Stabilization attempts would have been encouraged and necessary adjustment postponed. Although time-series forecasts tend to respond too much to current surprises, urging too much adjustment, the Bank's forecasts tended to be unresponsive to news, with previous predictions retained as long as possible and with relatively little shading in response to past failures.

The forecasts for copper and cotton are consistently less accurate than those for cocoa and coffee, and it is worth noting that the World

21

Bank did not have structural models for copper prior to 1985 or for cotton prior to 1988. Forecasts were largely driven by the Bank's predictions for inflation, exchange rates, and levels of gross domestic product (GDP), all of which were typically overoptimistic and which contained none of the mean reversion that appears in at least some of the models based more explicitly on supply and demand. While cotton prices continued along a constant trend from 1970 to 1980, the forecasts went with them, but the subsequent decline was not captured, and the predictions of a forthcoming (but never realized) boom have only slowly been shaded downward. Until the mid-1980s, future copper prices were almost always overestimated, and by amounts that seem very large. Copper-producing countries would have designed very poor policies had they acted on the basis of these predictions, quite apart from the misallocations that would have followed from the evaluation of any project for which the rate of return depended on the future price of copper. Indeed, several authors have commented on the effects of the overoptimistic copper-price forecasts on policy in Zambia (Powell, 1991; Aron, 1992).

Forecasts and Stabilization Policy: An Evaluation

It would be useful to compile a comparison of structural and time-series forecasts for a more complete list of commodities so that terms-of-trade predictions can be constructed for individual countries. The illustrations given here, however, should be enough to show that both methodologies have problems and that neither has been a reliable guide for the choice between stabilization or adjustment. The question therefore arises as to whether it is possible to do better, and what guidance can be given to policymakers about what should be done in the absence of reliable forecasts. In particular, is it possible to derive any set of automatic rules for responding to commodity-price shocks?

For several writers, the permanent-income theory of consumption has served as a useful model for stabilization, with consumption being held steady as prices and income fluctuate and reserves being built up in good times and run down in bad. A behavioral rule that sets consumption equal to permanent income, however, makes no allowance for precautionary motives or, in the absence of perfect international capital markets, for the investment that is required for growth. Furthermore, it is clear that such a rule works best when commodity income is serially uncorrelated and when there are no restrictions on the amounts that countries can borrow on international capital markets. Even if borrowing is limited—as it is in practice—it is still possible to accumulate a reserve fund, and although there will now be occasions when the absence of reserves forces a cut in consumption in response to a temporary income shortfall, consumption will still be a good deal smoother than income, and this can be achieved with relatively small levels of reserves. Deaton (1991) derives such buffer-stock rules and shows how they operate in practice. However, positive autocorrelation in income seriously compromises the performance of such stabilization schemes. Booms and slumps last much longer, so that to achieve the same degree of stabilization, larger amounts have to be accumulated during the boom and held for longer periods of time. Large reserves are costly; it is thus no longer desirable to stabilize as much, and consumption has to move more closely with income. In the limit, when income is a random walk, no stabilization is possible. It is doubtful that these results are much affected if we allow access to international capital markets; with strong positive autocorrelation, misfortune lasts for long and uncertain periods of time, and lenders are unlikely to wish to provide funds for stabilization under such circumstances.

The crucial point here has been previously argued by Gersovitz and Paxson (1990) and, in the context of attempts to stabilize farmers' incomes, by Newbery (1989). Given the actual behavior of commodity prices, which are very strongly autocorrelated at high frequencies and revert to their means only very slowly, it is quixotic to recommend any simple permanent-income rule or compensation scheme (as in Balassa, 1988). The swings are too wide, too long lived, and too uncertain. The accumulation of reserves over booms would be very large, very expensive, and almost certainly politically infeasible. Corresponding loans are not likely to be available over slumps; the amounts required would be very large and the repayment dates uncertain, or possibly infinite, if what was thought to be a downturn turned out to be a trend. The degree of persistence in commodity prices severely limits the scope for stabilization policy, so that price movements typically require rapid fundamental adjustment.

The exceptions to this argument are those cases in which it is clear *ex ante* that the price change will be short lived. Even in these instances, it is necessary to be careful. The frost in Brazil in 1975 that precipitated the coffee-price boom looks like a good example of such an event, and it is often cited as a clear case in which policymakers should have known that the shock would be temporary. Yet the World Bank forecasts underestimated both the effects and duration of the boom until the price had reached its peak in 1977. And the effect of the weather is not quite so clear as it may seem. A frost in Brazil in 1972 had almost as severe an effect—a 40 percent crop loss as opposed to 59 percent in 1975, and with a larger fall in world output, 18 percent as opposed to 15 percent—and yet there was no subsequent price flare. Temporary fluctuations are also frequently and "authoritatively" interpreted as permanent. Gasoline shortages and price increases in the United States in 1979–80 following the second oil shock were interpreted by some as a permanent consequence of the world running out of exhaustible resources. The hot summers from 1988 to 1991 in North America did much to persuade people of the inevitability of global warming. Popular perceptions, however plausible, are often wrong, and it is frequently difficult to determine the reasons for price changes even long after the event. There is danger in attempting to protect local prices against fluctuations in international prices, even when it *seems* clear that such fluctuations are temporary.

It should also be noted that most fluctuations in commodity prices have not been of a clearly temporary nature, and it is perhaps unfortunate that the coffee-price boom of the late 1970s should have so dominated the discussion. It is clear that the coffee-funded booms in government expenditures in Ivory Coast (Balassa, 1988) and Kenya (Bevan, Collier, and Gunning, 1990) were less-than-sensible responses to a boom that was (perhaps) widely understood to be of finite duration. The treatment of the subsequent slump in prices as temporary, however, and the consequent slowness in adopting adjustment policies was a reaction that was equally widely supported—by the World Bank and others—but that turned out to be just as wrong. The recent slumps in many prices, and their failure to turn into long-forecast booms, are better and more typical examples of the persistence and unforecastability of prices.

To the extent that policymakers need forecasts of commodity prices, perhaps most importantly for project evaluation, the lesson from the long-term data, which is captured by neither the simple time-series results nor (at least some of) the World Bank predictions, is that prices tend to revert to their long-term levels. Their real value is thus not likely to be higher for any prolonged period in the long-term future and may be lower if the trend pessimists are right. Although there is still dispute about long-term trends, the trend, if present, is not large relative to variability, so that the important thing is not to be misled by booms and slumps into predicting any major change in long-term values.

If such a view is correct, why is it not captured by the structural models? A definitive answer cannot be given, and we have only a very fragmentary understanding of the determinants of commodity prices in either the long or short term (see Deaton and Laroque, 1992, 1995, for evidence on the latter). One theory that seems consistent with the evidence goes back to Lewis (1954). Lewis noted that, despite substantial technical progress in the sugar industry, neither the price of sugar nor the wages of plantation workers had risen in real terms. He argued that, in the presence of unlimited supplies of workers at a low real wage, technical improvements in sugar production were passed on to consumers in rich countries in the form of lower prices and did not benefit the workers on the plantations. In this model, it is not the low prices of primary commodities that keeps wages low in the producing countries but rather the poverty in the developing countries that keeps commodity prices low. The real price of cocoa will increase permanently only when the opportunity cost of land and labor in the producing countries rises. By this reasoning, the production of staples cannot by itself engender development; rather, increases in the prices of staples must await development. In the long run, price is equal to marginal cost.

Despite the simplicity of Lewis's account, its features do not seem to be captured by any of the structural models. For example, Bateman (1990) predicts a new cocoa-price boom early in the next century. He points out that the prolonged low level of prices has led to an absence of replanting and to a slow decline in the size of the world's orchard. Meanwhile, demand is expanding; when it eventually outstrips supply, prices will rise. But such an analysis is self-contradictory; if it were correct, it would be undone by new planting four to five years prior to the anticipated price increase—with the Malaysians as the aggressive new producers most likely to make the arbitrage. But such responses are not included in the model, and we suspect that structural models of commodity prices, like their macroeconometric cousins, do not give sufficient recognition to the importance of expectations.

Is it possible to distill from all of this a simple policy rule for dealing with fluctuations in world commodity prices? In principle, given a description of the stochastic process driving prices, of the opportunities for capital formation and asset transactions, and of an appropriate social-welfare function, there will exist an optimal policy function that embodies a set of rules for responding to any given contingency. In practice, the calculations are not feasible, and we can only guess at the nature of the solution. To the extent that the sharp upward spikes in commodity prices are driven by clearly stationary shocks, such as abnormal weather conditions or industrial disputes, it makes sense to try to smooth them out, not to adjust consumption and investment, and to accumulate the proceeds in a compensation fund the balance of which can be used to fund consumption and investment over the long term. It is in this case that the permanent-income rule is appropriate. Except in such cases, however, where the temporary nature of the shocks can be clearly and unambiguously identified, price changes should be treated as if they were permanent, and fundamental adjustments made. Although it is typically the case that prices will eventually revert to their long-term norms, the process is so long and so uncertain that attempts to ignore fluctuations by holding consumption and investment on their long-term growth paths are doomed to fail. Rather than reacting to commodity-price uncertainty after the fact, governments may do better by trying to eliminate at least some of the uncertainty by using futures, options, and swaps, instruments that are currently under active review by the World Bank and by the producer countries themselves.

3 THE POLITICAL ECONOMY OF TAXATION AND EXPENDITURE IN AFRICA

Even had commodity prices been easier to forecast, the responses of African governments to commodity-price shocks might still have been less than ideal judged from the viewpoint of growth and stabilization. This chapter looks at the fiscal arrangements of African commodity exporters and at the forces determining levels of taxation and government expenditures and asks whether these arrangements are likely to affect the response of African countries to fluctuations in the prices of their exports. There is a well-developed economic theory of what taxes ought to be in these countries and a substantial political-economic literature that aims to explain why taxes are what they are. Sometimes the two views coincide, but frequently they do not, and it is widely believed that the internal organization of taxation and expenditure, as influenced by the political environment, has a great deal to do with difficulties in selecting appropriate stabilization policies. We review some of this literature, with a view both to identifying directions of policy reform and to identifying hypotheses to be examined in the subsequent empirical work.

The argument runs as follows. Even from a purely economic perspective, it is desirable to tax commodity exports, a prescription that is followed in most (but not all) African countries. Tax rates are frequently hard to explain by reference to either equity or efficiency, however, even allowing for administrative constraints, and are perhaps better explained by political factors. As a result of high commodity taxes, levied by paying low and inflexible procurement prices to farmers, fluctuations in world prices lead to proportionately larger fluctuations in government revenue. In general, governments in Africa are revenue constrained, and they have no direct control over the large portions of government expenditure that are financed by foreign donors. Because revenue from commodity booms is in some cases the only income over which governments have complete discretion, much of it is used, not for economic growth, but for constituency building and the consolidation of power.

If such arguments are accepted, an important question for discussion is whether, at the same average level of taxation, arrangements that share income fluctuations more evenly between public and private sectors might not lead to superior stabilization outcomes. We deal with these questions below, looking first at the level of taxation and then at the performance of tax systems through booms and slumps in international prices.

The Level of Commodity Taxation

The economic theory of taxation and public expenditure pays little attention to political factors but nevertheless provides recommendations that overlap in a number of areas with what actually happens. The optimal level of taxation on agricultural exports is not zero. Most African governments have only a limited choice of tax instruments, so that given a revenue requirement, the question is not whether cocoa or coffee should be taxed, but at what rates. There is a standard set of rules for determining these rates, balancing equity against efficiency and taking into account the availability of alternative instruments of taxation. Newbery (1990) provides an excellent discussion in the context of cocoa pricing in Ghana, using what little evidence exists on the supply responses of cocoa farmers (substantial in the long term) and on their position with respect to income distribution (worse-off than urban consumers of imports, better-off than much of the rural population). In the case of tree crops, Newbery's largely static analysis has to be modified by the intertemporal issues that arise from the fact that once the orchard exists, at least some output can be obtained at very low cost. Besley (1992) shows that such circumstances can set a lower bound on taxes if farmers are faced by a predatory government or marketing board. If the board attempts to set too high a price, one that would induce a substantial expansion of the orchard, the farmers will calculate that the board will subsequently have an eventually irresistible incentive to reduce prices to marginal production costs, even if in so doing, there will never again be any new planting. As a result, only prices below a critical level are credible and will induce new investment.

Economic arguments also favor the use of at least some of the tax revenue for government investment projects. In the standard literature on project evaluation, the government acts as a representative for future generations, and money in the hands of the government is committed to the investment projects that have the highest yield. The taxation of agriculture to advance industrial development, a policy that was favored by most economists into the 1970s and that fit well with the political needs of many African leaders, could be seen as the implementation of an optimal intertemporal allocation condition, equating the marginal value of funds between present and future consumption.

28

Although there is nothing inherently wrong with export taxes or with taxation for investment, the details are very different from those recommended by economic theory. Some countries have set tax rates at levels that seem hard to justify from an economic perspective. Newbery (1990) documents the way confiscatory rates on cocoa in Ghana gradually destroyed the industry by the early 1980s. Although cocoa and coffee farmers will still harvest their crops in the face of low prices, they will not replant, and the orchard will slowly diminish (the structural-adjustment program begun in Ghana in 1983 has done much toward reversing this trend). Ivory Coast, which is often taken as the example that Ghana should emulate, has consistently paid farmers the same amount for cocoa and coffee, although coffee costs almost twice as much to produce as cocoa in Ivory Coast, although the world price of coffee has usually been higher (see Figure 1), and although Ivory Coast has some power over the world market in cocoa but none in coffee (Benjamin and Deaton, 1993). As a result, coffee in Ivory Coast has suffered much the same fate as cocoa in Ghana. Furthermore, the policy of keeping producer prices constant in real terms, with substantial implicit taxation, had to be abandoned in 1989—and producer prices eventually cut by half—when declines in world prices turned taxes into subsidies.

It is in the recommendations for taxation and public investment, however, that the (once) standard economic prescriptions seem naive, particularly in their implicit assumptions that (1) private individuals are unlikely to save or, if they save at all, are unlikely to make sensible investment decisions, and (2) governments will act as effective custodians of the future, investing wisely and applying project-evaluation guidelines to guarantee equitable and efficient growth. In practice, with tax rates poorly set and projects selected on other than economic grounds, great damage has been done to agriculture with little compensating benefit elsewhere in the economy.

Of course, these broad generalizations are just that and fit some countries much better than others. Kenya, unlike Ghana or Ivory Coast, has typically not taxed the incomes of the smallholder coffee producers, and even during the coffee-price boom, the windfall was not taxed, a decision reputedly made personally by President Jomo Kenyatta, against the advice of both the IMF and the World Bank (Killick, 1984). There is surely no economic reason for tax policies to vary so much from country to country, and the explanation of the differences must lie in differences in political structures. Indeed, many writers have emphasized the role of ethnic divisions in Africa, and the relation between the level of taxation and the extent to which the farmers are politically represented. Bates (1989) notes that where independence was spearheaded by farmers in search of land (Kenya) or better prices (Ivory Coast), subsequent policy has been more favorable to agricultural interests (see also Bates, 1981, 1983; Lofchie, 1989). In Ghana, Kwame Nkrumah and subsequent leaders have drawn their support from urban groups and have typically been hostile to both private-sector and agricultural interests, a pattern that is repeated in many other countries. As a result, the Ashanti farmers who grow cocoa in Ghana have had no political representation and see their government as being dominated by other interests. Indeed, the attempt in 1954 by the National Liberation Movement to mobilize political opposition around farmer and Ashanti interests was quickly outmaneuvered and suppressed by Nkrumah (Frimpong-Ansah, 1992). In Nigeria, too, ethnicity is linked to specific crops; cocoa is grown by the Yoruba in the west, groundnuts by the Hausa in the north, and palm products by the Ibo in the east. None of these farming interests is well represented politically in comparison with industrial, bureaucratic, and military interests (Bienen, 1988). In Senegal, by contrast, groundnuts in Senegal are grown by the Mourides, a politically powerful and well-organized ethnic group that has successfully prevented high taxation of its crops (Bates, 1983).

Many African leaders adopted the standard economic prescription of industrialization funded from agricultural taxation, if sometimes more in rhetoric than reality; see, for example, Frimpong-Ansah's (1992) account of Ghana under Nkrumah. There are other cases and other motivations, however. Many (although not all) first-generation African leaders had no natural political constituency, and the revenue from taxation could be used to build one. The investment projects that would engender economic development could also be used to make new friends and reward old ones. Indeed, it is a commonplace among observers that rate-of-return calculations play little or no role in project evaluation in Africa—or in much of the world (Squire, 1989); economic growth is at best only one of many objectives motivating those who authorize and fund development expenditures. Nigeria is perhaps only the most egregious and well-documented example (although see also the discussion in Bevan, Collier, and Gunning, 1990, of the disintegration of public-expenditure management in Kenya after the coffee boom). In Nigeria, there was an uncontrolled explosion of public projects in the wake of the oil booms (Bienen, 1988; Gavin, 1993). In 1984, the Federal Military Government appointed a committee, subsequently known as the Onosode Committee, to review these and other projects. The committee found that virtually no public-sector projects were supported even by attempts to measure rates of return, and it recommended—as did the World Bank and the U.S. government—that a number of partly completed major public projects be abandoned. Among these was the infamous Ajaokuta steel works, which is situated far from the sea, where transport is difficult and where there are neither energy sources nor supplies of iron ore. Work on many of these projects still continues, and Ajaokuta was recently proclaimed by its project director, without apparent irony, as a model "for the future of the black man all over the world" ("Nigeria's Monumental Steel Plant: Nationalist Mission or Colossal Mistake?" *New York Times*, July 11, 1992). This and other projects exist, not because of their contribution to economic development, but because of the political benefits that they bring to their sponsors.

It might be thought that giving farmers good prices for their crops would also help build political support. But, as emphasized by Bates (1983), this is often less effective. It is difficult to build support across ethnic divisions, and although the benefits of high prices accrue indiscriminately to all producers, projects can be steered so as to reward friends and punish enemies. The same logic leads to a reluctance to devalue national currencies. Although overvalued exchange rates tax agricultural producers, they also offer the opportunity for import controls, which, like projects, provide many occasions for channeling favors to urban clients. Because politically powerful large farmers can be bought off with fertilizer subsidies, the burden of agricultural taxation falls only on the relatively poor smallholders who use little or no marketed inputs. There has been little evidence of anything other than a rhetorical commitment to equity in African pricing policies.

Taxation in Booms and Slumps

High taxes on agricultural exports frequently—though, again, not universally—take the form of marketing boards setting procurement prices that not only are lower than world prices, but are also unresponsive to changes in world prices. Because most African countries have insufficient power over world prices to induce a negative correlation between output and price, these relatively fixed prices have the effect of stabilizing farmers' incomes. Indeed, income stabilization is frequently the declared purpose of the parastatal procurement agencies. Of course, stabilization of farmers' incomes comes at the price of destabilizing government revenues. Because the issue of the level of taxation is conceptually distinct from the allocation of income fluctuations, it is

31

possible at the same level of average taxation to imagine different arrangements for the sharing of fluctuations. The same average level of tax can be levied as a land tax, independent of the level of output or value of sales; as a specific tax, on the physical volume of sales; or as an *ad valorem* tax, on the value of sales. Alternatively, governments can announce prices on a year-by-year basis, which permits, for example, progressive taxation with a larger fraction withheld during booms than during slumps; in the past, when Thailand was dependent on rice exports, the rice "premium" was reduced when prices were low and increased when prices were high. Just as the *level* of taxes varies across Africa, so does the extent to which farm-gate prices vary with world prices, and thus so does the extent to which revenue booms and slumps are allocated between the farmers and the government.

There are two distinct issues here, one normative and one positive. First, there is the essentially microeconomic question of the desirability or undesirability of stabilizing farmers' incomes, ignoring any problems the government might have in handling fluctuations in its own revenue. Second, there is the macroeconomic stabilization issue that comes from comparing the actual saving and investment behavior of farmers with that of the government. There is a wide dispersion of views on these matters, and there has been controversy for at least half a century.

The stabilization of farmers' incomes was used by the British colonial administration as at least one of the arguments for establishing marketing boards. The cases for and against the boards were well put as early as the debate between Bauer and Paish (1952) and Friedman (1954). The former argued against the use of marketing boards as instruments of taxation, proposing instead a form of moving-average payment, on the grounds that "small producers are unlikely to have the self-restraint and foresight to set aside in good times sufficient reserves to cushion the effects of worse ones, or, even if they have, may be debarred from doing so by social customs and obligations (p. 766)." Friedman, in reply, emphasized the forced-saving aspects of the scheme and doubted whether marketing boards were a suitable substitute for education and the development of credit markets. It is certainly correct that, if saving is ignored and it is assumed that farmers are forced to consume their incomes, then it is desirable for the government to shoulder some of the risk by stabilizing prices; under reasonable assumptions, such stabilization can be substantial (Mirrlees, 1988). Note, however, that as argued by Newbery (1989), the persistence of commodity-price movements generates difficulties for this sort of stabilization, just as it does for macroeconomic stabilization.

That farmers misspend boom incomes is a widely held view. Frimpong-Ansah (1992, p. 71) quotes a British Colonial Office memorandum of 1944, which describes the consequences of farmers receiving boom incomes after World War I, as "almost wholly evil. They received more money than they knew what to do with. . . . [They developed] exaggerated ideas of the value of their products, and numerous expensive tastes were acquired." More recently, Davis (1983) recommends stabilization on macroeconomic grounds, on equity grounds, and because there will otherwise be excessive planting in response to the temporarily high prices. These views are echoed by Killick (1984, p. 179) for Kenya, who writes of the 1978–80 coffee boom that, "in terms of economic management, there was an overwhelming case for preventing all the windfall gains from accruing to the farmers. These were purely windfall profits, in no sense a return on past investments, and they were large in relation to domestic demand. Alone among the major producing countries, Kenya did not tax coffee revenues."

The contrary case is argued in terms of what happens when the government gets the revenue, particularly in terms of its tendency to spend it on ill-conceived public projects. Hirschman (1977) argues from the Peruvian guano boom, as well as from many more recent episodes, that "fiscal linkages" to staples are unlikely to promote worthwhile investment and growth. Bevan, Collier, and Gunning (1990) believe that the Kenyan government's ability to vet investment projects was permanently compromised by the scramble for projects in the wake of the coffee boom. Even though the authorities understood perfectly well what was happening, the obvious availability of funds made it impossible to control spending departments, which refused to rank projects so as to prevent the Ministry of Finance from exercising fiscal control. It is important to note that the Kenyan authorities received nothing directly from the coffee boom; the increase in government revenues was the secondary effect of the inflation of other sources of revenue, primarily imports. Nigeria is an example where the fragility of the federal structure, with "a continuous struggle between regional autonomy and central control," (Bienen, 1988, p. 232) makes it difficult to prevent the rapid and uncontrolled disbursement of discretionary incomes. The transitory nature of the recent mini oil boom associated with the Kuwaiti war was well understood by the Nigerian authorities, but the revenues were immediately spent nevertheless, in spite of explicit prior presidential announcements to the contrary (Gavin, 1993).

There are arguments in favor of leaving stabilization to the farmers. At the microeconomic level, much depends on the empirical evidence

33

about whether smallholders can make sensible intertemporal choices. The evidence on this, although far from complete, is relatively favorable. Hill (1963, p. 181), in her classic study of Ghanaian cocoa producers, writes of the migrant cocoa growers that "the farmers were prepared to take their time and held as rigid a view as many old-fashioned capitalists or communists as to the wastefulness of consumption expenditure." Ingham (1973) presents some empirical evidence that supports such a view. Bevan, Collier, and Gunning (1989) use rather fragmentary but internally consistent macroeconomic and microeconomic evidence from Kenya to suggest that farmers fully understood the temporary nature of the coffee boom and that they saved about 60 percent of the proceeds. Later evidence from other countries is more mixed but is consistent with the view that farmers will save from income that is clearly perceived as transitory (Collier and Gunning, 1994, 1995).

There is also more formal evidence from other countries that farmers can handle income uncertainty very well. Perhaps the most convincing studies are those by Paxson (1992, 1993) of Thai rice farmers, who smooth their consumption both within and between harvest years. Bauer (1984) also argues that farmers in developing countries are likely to invest well, using boom income not only to expand their orchards, but to diversify into money lending, transportation, and processing activities, many of which have high rates of return (for a more detailed analysis of such linkages, see Hirschman, 1977). Bevan, Collier, and Gunning (1990) conclude their study of Kenya and Tanzania with a manifesto for policy that contrasts the "good" behavior of farmers with the "bad" behavior of governments. It should be noted, however—and this is one of the main points of the analysis by Bevan, Collier, and Gunning—that even "good" behavior by farmers can be frustrated by Dutch-disease effects or by an otherwise hostile macroeconomic environment, particularly if there are physical controls. If the government limits access to foreign exchange, the private sector cannot directly hold windfall balances abroad. Controls on imports will generate domestic inflation, redistribute income from the rural to the urban sector, and undermine incentives for agricultural producers; government actions may thus abort what otherwise could have been a successful investment boom.

Many of these arguments seem worth treating seriously, as does the policy implication that governments should be encouraged, even when the level of taxation is not easily negotiated, to adjust the tax regime so as to allow the private sector a larger share in stabilizing fluctuations in commodity incomes. The effectiveness of such a policy is likely to be much enhanced if other reforms are undertaken simultaneously, particularly the dismantling of physical controls. Such steps seem desirable even if progress is made on what is perhaps the most important issue, which is finding some way of improving the quality of project evaluation. Of course, we are still at the stage of evaluating proposals based on their inherent logic and on analogies with experience elsewhere. The hard empirical evidence with which to support or contradict these positions for Africa is simply not available. In a first attempt to gather that evidence, the next two chapters offer econometric results that attempt to assess how commodity-price fluctuations have affected Sub-Saharan Africa as a whole.

4 PAN-AFRICAN EMPIRICAL EVIDENCE

Data and Empirical Methodology

Data from Africa are typically incomplete, error ridden, and inconsistent across different authorities. The results presented here use data from several different international sources, and the numbers are sometimes contradictory or otherwise suspect. In consequence, the results should be treated with even more than the usual degree of caution. The object of our exercise is to examine the effects of changes in commodity prices on the components of national income, consumption, investment, government expenditure, and net exports. We use an extended vector autoregression (VARX) in which GDP and its components are each regressed on their own lags and on the contemporaneous and lagged values of an index of international commodity prices specific to each country.

The base national-income data come from the Penn World Table (Mark 5.6), the first release of which is described in Summers and Heston (1991). We extract data from 1958 to 1992 for the thirty-two Sub-Saharan African countries listed in Table 3; depending on the availability of other series, we use various subsets of these data. The standard measure of national income recommended by Summers and Heston, the measure routinely used in the recent explosion of empirical work on economic growth, is a chain-index measure of real national output. It is important to note that this is an *output* measure of GDP, not an *income* measure. In particular, if there is a boom in the world price of a country's main export, there will be no direct effect on the GDP measure, even though the country's output will now buy a larger volume of goods and services on international markets. The Penn World Table also provides data on GDP corrected for terms-of-trade effects that incorporate the real-income effects of changes in the terms of trade. The results reported below, however, use only the output data, so that any commodity-price effects on national income represent real changes in the volume of output as a result of the price changes. For example, if producers use their windfall earnings for investment, and the investment goods are imported from abroad, investment will show an increase, net exports will show a compensating decrease, and GDP will remain unchanged. It is only when investment (or something else) elicits new output that an effect of commodity prices on GDP will be detected.

A measure of export prices is constructed for each of the thirty-two countries by weighting the international commodity-price data in the IMF's *International Financial Statistics* (1994) by fixed export weights specific to each country. This is preferable to using export unit values, which are affected by the composition of exports and, thus, by what happens to GDP and its components. Much of the cross-country empirical work on growth is plagued by endogeneity problems, and one of the great advantages of using international commodity prices is that they are typically unaffected by the behavior of individual countries. In some instances, countries may have a limited market power (Ivory Coast and Ghana in cocoa, for example; Madagascar in vanilla and cloves; Kenya and Tanzania in sisal; Senegal in groundnut oil; Guinea in bauxite; Zambia in copper; Gabon in manganese; Botswana and Zaire in diamonds; and Zaire in cobalt), but cases in which countries have deliberately and successfully manipulated the markets have been rare. Problems will still occur when an exogenous shock, for example a miners' strike in Zambia, simultaneously affects both the country's GDP and the world price of the commodity. Even so, exogeneity is a reasonable assumption as a first approximation.

The export prices used here are constructed as follows. Twenty-one commodities are distinguished, partly on grounds of importance, but also partly because of data availability; they are:

cocoa (COC), coffee (COF), cotton (COT), groundnuts (GRO), groundnut oil (GNO), oilpalm products (OLP), rubber (RUB), sisal (SIS), sugar (SUG), tea (TEA), tobacco (TOB), wool (WOO), bauxite (BAU), copper (COP), gold (GOL), iron (IRO), manganese (MAN), nickel (NIC), oil (OIL), phosphates (PHO), uranium (URA)

For each of the countries, we calculate the total value of exports of the twenty-one commodities in 1975 and weight them by dividing the value of each commodity's exports in 1975 by this total. These weights are then held fixed over time and are applied to the world prices of the same commodities (taken from *International Financial Statistics*) to form a geometrically weighted index of prices. The commodities for each country and their weights in 1975 exports are given in Table 3. Because the nature and composition of each country's exports differed from one another in 1975, the commodity-price indices move differently for each country, even though the underlying world prices of the twenty-one commodities are the same. We make no attempt to allow for the fact that different countries may receive different prices for their products, by quota sales through commodity-price agreements, for

TABLE 3

DISTRIBUTION OF AFRICAN COUNTRY EXPORTS IN 1975
(percent of country's total value of exports)

	COC	COF	COT	GRO	GNO	OLP	RUB	SIS	SUG	TEA	TOB	WOO	BAU	COP	GOL	IRO	MAN	NIC	OIL	PHO	URA
Benin	17.8	4.0	42.8	5.9		23.0					6.4										
Botswana														17.5				82.6			
Burkina Faso			47.2	44.6					8.3												
Burundi		95.8	1.7							2.5											
Cameroon	52.1	37.5	2.7	2.1		1.4	3.6		0.1	0.2	0.6										
C.A.R.	0.7	53.2	40.3				1.3				4.5										
Congo	2.0	0.6				0.2			2.0		0.4			1.2					93.7		
Ethiopia		85.4	4.6	2.4					7.7												
Gabon	0.3	0.0				0.0											9.7		88.8		1.2
The Gambia				62.8	34.9	2.3															
Ghana	81.0	0.4				0.0					0.1		4.2		12.3		2.2				
Ivory Coast	43.7	45.1	2.6			7.4	1.2														
Kenya		50.9	2.0			0.0		13.2	0.1	33.1		0.6									
Lesotho												100.0									
Liberia	1.3	1.3				0.7	13.2									83.6					
Madagascar	1.5	64.1	0.0	2.0				9.7	21.7		1.0										
Malawi		0.3	2.0	6.6					12.4	22.0	56.7										
Mali			87.9	10.2					0.8	1.1											
Mauritania														6.8		93.2					
Mauritius									99.0	1.0											
Niger		0.1	0.0	7.9					0.8												91.2

Nigeria	4.3	0.0	0.0		0.1	0.3							95.2
Rwanda	87.9						12.1						
Senegal		2.3	2.3		2.3	0.0							38.8
Sierra Leone	24.5	19.7	54.3		9.1				10.0		36.6		
Sudan	65.0	33.6	1.0				0.3						
Tanzania	0.4	30.6	18.7	37.9	0.0	2.1	5.1	5.2					
Togo	19.0	7.1	0.9		2.6	0.2							70.2
Uganda	0.1	79.2	10.1				6.7	0.9		3.1			
Zaire	1.0	16.5	0.1		3.6	1.8	0.6			73.5	2.6	0.4	
Zambia										98.9	1.1		
Zimbabwe	1.3	12.0			1.8		34.5	34.5					15.9

NOTE: Numbers are rounded and may not add to 100. Important commodities excluded for lack of data are diamonds (Botswana, Sierra Leone), lumber (Cameroon, Ghana), gum arabic (Sudan), chrome (Sierra Leone), vanilla and cloves (Madagascar), beef (Botswana), and cobalt (Zaire); an entry of 0.0 indicates inclusion of commodity at less than one-tenth of 1 percent.

SOURCES: Most shares are computed from 1975 export values given in UN, *Yearbook of International Trade Statistics* (1978). Data for Lesotho come from UN (UNCTAD), *Handbook of International Trade and Development Statistics* (1978); for a few of the smaller entries not listed in UN sources, data are calculated from physical-quantity export data from World Bank, *African Economic and Financial Data* (1990). The prices for all but groundnuts and uranium come from IMF, *International Financial Statistics* (1994); those prices that are closest to a world price included in *International Financial Statistics* are selected, with the African option used whenever possible, e.g., Ugandan coffee prices in New York, Ghanian cocoa in London, East African sisal, Sudanese cotton, and Moroccan phosphate. The uranium price series comes from American Metal Market, *Metal Statistics* (1978) and from Radetski, *Uranium: A Strategic Source of Energy* (1981), and are spot prices on the NUEXCO exchange for U_3O_8; the price series for groundnuts comes from splicing together a series from *International Financial Statistics* with data for 1975–76 from the *FAO Quarterly Bulletin of Statistics* and subsequent data from the *UNCTAD Commodity Yearbook*. The FAO and UNCTAD series are conceptually identical and are equal in years of overlapping availability. The IMF data appear unreasonable for the 1980s and do not match well with those from UNCTAD for that decade.

example, or by selling forward through agents. The weights are held fixed over time because we are trying to construct a variable that is exogenous and that cannot therefore include any supply responses to world prices. As a result, we lose some important windfall events, such as the discovery of oil in Cameroon in 1975 with production coming on line in 1978 (one of the episodes included in the Collier-Gunning comparative study). The loss is inevitable, however, if we are to exclude other, clearly endogenous quantity changes. (It is also not obvious that the effects of output windfalls must be similar to those of price windfalls.) Even with fixed weights, exogeneity is threatened to the extent that countries have market power in individual commodities.

Note that the list of twenty-one commodities is far from comprehensive. The omission of diamonds for Botswana is perhaps the most glaring deficiency (Table 3 shows Botswana's 1975 exports as 82.6 percent nickel and 17.5 percent copper). There are many other omissions, however, some of which are listed in the notes to the table. Like diamonds, these exclusions are forced on us by the inability to obtain useful prices. The resulting price indices will typically be correlated with the true (complete) price indices for each country, but the omissions will make the proxy less than perfect and will therefore tend to bias toward zero the estimated effects of commodity prices. Before inclusion in the VARX, the commodity-price index is deflated by the World Bank's index of imports of manufactured goods by developing countries. It should be noted that Somalia is the one Sub-Saharan country in the Penn World Table that exported none of the above-listed twenty-one commodities in 1975; it is therefore dropped from the analysis.

There are four equations in the system, for real GDP, for consumption, for investment, and for government expenditure, all expressed in logarithms. Logarithms are convenient in that the parameters can be interpreted as elasticities, but they are less convenient when it comes to respecting the linear national-accounting identities. Because the four magnitudes, consumption, investment, government expenditure, and net exports, add up to the fifth, GDP, we can in principle choose any four for the system, with the fifth being determined by the identity. In logarithms, the identity cannot hold exactly, and it would matter which subset were selected if the choice were not determined by the fact that net exports can be negative and so cannot appear in a logarithmic system. In each equation, the current value is regressed on three lags of itself and three lags of each of the other three variables in the system, together with the contemporaneous value and three lags of a measure of the price of commodity exports. Country-specific effects and trends are accommodated by including country-specific dummies and time trends. (An alternative method is to run the regressions in first differences with country-specific intercepts; the results of that method are explored below as part of our tests of robustness.) There are twenty-three observations (from 1961 to 1986, less the three years lost to lags) for each of the thirty-two countries. Estimation is by the "seemingly unrelated regression" (SUR) methodology, so that first-stage ordinary least-squares (OLS) regressions are used to estimate a variance-covariance matrix of the residuals, which in turn is used to calculate systemwide generalized least-squares (GLS) estimates at the second stage. The distinction between OLS and SUR methods has no major impact on the results; the real issue here is not how the residuals are treated but whether behavior is homogeneous across countries, a question to which we shall return below.

Baseline Results on the Effects of Commodity Prices on National Output

The baseline results are presented in Table 4, which gives the coefficients on commodity prices (the last four rows) together with the coefficients on the system lags. Numbers highlighted are significantly different from zero, or nearly so, and large enough to be important. Because the results are close enough to what might be expected, we can perhaps resist claims that the data are so error ridden as to be useless. Nevertheless, there are a number of surprises. Let us start from the VAR estimates in the top twelve rows of the table. GDP and its three components are all strongly autoregressive, with at least the first lag of each entering significantly into its own equation. For all the equations, there are partly offsetting effects in the second and third lags. The most important cross-effect in the VARX is of lagged GDP on investment, which is echoed by a smaller but significant effect of lagged investment on GDP, suggesting a traditional multiplier-accelerator model. For a country that invests 20 percent of GDP, investment of $1,000 increases the next year's GDP by $130; as the effects work through the system, this falls to $102 in the second year, $30 in the third year, and becomes negative for several years thereafter. In this system, the ultimate effect of any innovation, whether investment or commodity prices, is zero, because it is assumed by construction that the system is stationary around deterministic trends. Clearly, this is only an assumption and may well be incorrect. These data are not likely to be informative about long-term effects, and the results should

41

TABLE 4

COMMODITY PRICES AND COMPONENTS OF GDP: EXTENDED
VECTOR AUTOREGRESSIONS (VARX)

	GDP	Consumption	Investment	Government Expenditure
$\ln y_{t-1}$	0.91 (10.9)	0.15 (1.3)	0.65 (1.9)	0.10 (0.6)
$\ln y_{t-2}$	0.08 (0.8)	0.23 (1.6)	−0.16 (0.4)	−0.20 (1.0)
$\ln y_{t-3}$	−0.16 (2.0)	−0.07 (0.7)	−0.05 (0.2)	0.14 (0.9)
$\ln c_{t-1}$	−0.11 (2.2)	0.54 (7.3)	−0.07 (0.3)	−0.04 (0.4)
$\ln c_{t-2}$	−0.06 (1.1)	−0.13 (1.4)	−0.02 (0.1)	0.11 (1.0)
$\ln c_{t-3}$	0.04 (0.7)	−0.09 (1.2)	0.09 (0.4)	−0.05 (0.5)
$\ln i_{t-1}$	0.03 (2.7)	0.04 (2.7)	0.61 (13.9)	0.03 (1.7)
$\ln i_{t-2}$	−0.02 (1.4)	−0.02 (1.6)	−0.03 (0.7)	0.02 (1.0)
$\ln i_{t-3}$	−0.01 (0.9)	−0.01 (0.7)	−0.13 (3.0)	−0.02 (1.0)
$\ln g_{t-1}$	0.00 (0.1)	0.02 (0.6)	−0.08 (0.7)	0.74 (14.5)
$\ln g_{t-2}$	−0.07 (2.3)	−0.12 (2.8)	−0.05 (0.4)	−0.01 (0.2)
$\ln g_{t-3}$	0.03 (1.2)	0.04 (1.2)	0.01 (0.1)	−0.11 (2.2)
$\ln p_t$	0.01 (0.6)	−0.00 (0.2)	0.10 (2.2)	−0.00 (0.2)
$\ln p_{t-1}$	0.04 (2.4)	0.05 (2.5)	0.09 (1.6)	0.05 (1.9)
$\ln p_{t-2}$	−0.01 (0.6)	−0.02 (0.8)	−0.05 (0.9)	0.00 (0.1)
$\ln p_{t-3}$	0.02 (1.7)	0.04 (2.2)	0.07 (1.5)	−0.02 (0.8)

NOTE: Estimated coefficients are from the SUR estimation of a
four-equation system of the logarithms of GDP, consumption, investment, and government expenditure. The SUR variance-covariance
matrix is estimated from first-stage OLS residuals. Different countries
are allowed to have different error variances but are constrained to
have the same correlation matrix of the cross-equation innovations.
Numbers in parentheses are absolute t-values.
SOURCE: Penn World Table (Mark 5.6), 1961–1986.

not be used to make inferences about dynamics more than a few years
into the future. They certainly are not capable of telling whether commodity booms permanently raise either GDP or its growth rate.

Changes in international commodity prices work most strongly
through investment. There are strong positive effects even contempora-
neously, and these are reinforced in the subsequent period, with some
offset in the third; the multiplier–accelerator links between investment
and GDP transmit this into output and into further increases in investment. There are also direct effects of commodity-price changes in the
previous period on consumption and government expenditure, and
although the two elasticities are the same, the absolute effects of the

price change on consumption are three times larger than they are on government expenditure, because consumption is, on average, three times larger than government expenditure. The allocation of effects between government expenditure and investment should not be treated too seriously. Although government expenditure in the Penn World Table is, in principle, government consumption, many statistical offices do not adhere to a uniform procedure for separating government investment from government consumption. Further, investment (and consumption) by parastatals (of which marketing boards are only one example) will not always be allocated to the government, even in cases in which it would be appropriate to do so.

The responses of national output and its components to a (non-maintained) shock to commodity prices are shown in Figure 5. These are shown, not in logarithms, but as actual changes expressed as shares of national output (y) and are approximated using the formula

$$\frac{\Delta x}{y} \approx \frac{x}{y} \Delta \ln x \ , \tag{7}$$

where x is consumption, investment, or government expenditure, and the shares of GDP are evaluated at the sample means and are 0.702 for consumption, 0.102 for investment, and 0.221 for government expenditure. The effects on net exports are calculated as a residual and so will include not only the genuine effects, but also any errors from the loglinear approximations. The effects on national output, consumption, investment, and government expenditure are relatively straightforward and follow fairly obviously from the coefficients in Table 4. The maximum effect on all five magnitudes is in periods one to three after the price shock. Beyond the second period, consumption, investment, government expenditure, and net imports remain higher than they would otherwise have been, and the effects die away slowly, although almost all are exhausted after five to seven years. Note, particularly, that the price increase generates a *fall* in net exports of 2 percent of GDP in the first year after the shock but tends back to zero thereafter. Again, it is important to recall that the direct positive effects on the balance of trade of the commodity-price increase are not included here, because all magnitudes are in volume terms. For the thirty-two countries considered, commodity exports were on average about 15 percent of GDP. The immediate positive price effects would, therefore, much more than offset the immediate negative volume effects that operate (presumably) through the additional imports supporting the increases in consumption and investment.

43

FIGURE 5

IMPULSE RESPONSE TO A COMMODITY-PRICE SHOCK

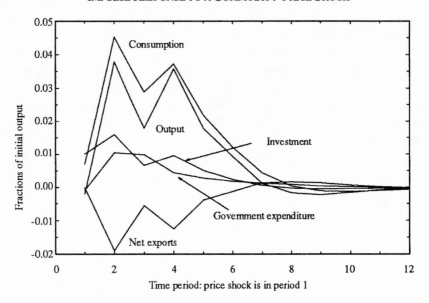

SOURCE: Authors' calculations as described in the text.

There are a number of caveats that should be entered at this point. First, it is worth reiterating that the split between government expenditure and investment is not to be trusted. Second, it is likely that some of the measured change in national output comes from labor (and other factors) moving in and out of unrecorded activities in agriculture and elsewhere. If government expenditure employs new workers whose previous activities fell outside the national-income net, measured national output will increase and decrease with government expenditure, although actual output may be moving not at all, or even perversely. Third, these results tell us very little about the *quality* of investment (or of government expenditure); these data and methods are not well suited to detecting the eventual declines in national output that might happen if low- or negative-return state projects crowd out high-return private projects as a commodity-price boom reallocates revenue toward government.

Even with all the difficulties in mind, however, the results show no evidence of a generally unsuccessful or clearly inappropriate response to commodity-price shocks, at least for the thirty-two countries as a group. Commodity-price booms have generally favorable effects on African economies; they stimulate investment and generate additional GDP. There is no obvious evidence that booms trigger a GDP decline, that windfalls are immediately converted into government expenditure at a rate of one for one or even higher, or that long-term trade imbalances linger beyond the initial effects of some of the windfall being used to pay for imports. Admittedly, the evidence is relatively weak, and there are doubtless some countries where horror stories have occurred. But the stories do not appear to generalize to all the countries in Sub-Saharan Africa.

Some Tests of Robustness

The baseline results are not reached without making assumptions about specifications and data, assumptions that might affect the outcome. This is true quite apart from the pervasive general doubts about data quality that hamper all such investigations in the African context. We therefore consider a number of alternative specifications and data choices to test the robustness of the results.

As stated, our baseline VARX regressions use national-accounting data from the Penn World Table (Mark 5.6), except for data for Uganda and Sudan, for which we use earlier versions of the Table. The commodity-price index for twenty-one commodity exports is deflated by an index of import prices for developing countries. The basic format assumes that the variables are trend stationary in logarithms and that country-specific intercepts and time trends are included in all the regressions. The equations are estimated by feasible generalized least-squares (FGLS) or SUR methods, under the assumption that error variances are constant over time but differ across countries. For the basic case in Table 4, the results do not differ by much if the equations are estimated by OLS rather than FGLS methods. Such differences as exist are largely in the timing, with the OLS regressions showing significant contemporaneous effects of the commodity-price index on national output and investment.

The FGLS estimation effectively assigns each country a weight that is proportional to the precision of the OLS estimates, with countries with small equation standard errors given greater weight than those for which the regression predicts poorly. This interpretation raises questions about alternative weighting schemes. One possibility is to weight countries by population, so that the results can be thought of as representative of African people rather than of a typical African country (whereby Nigeria or Sudan count no more than Gabon or Lesotho). Weighting the regressions by populations in 1975 generates largely similar results with somewhat greater contemporaneous impact. The effect on consumption is amplified, and that on investment is slightly attenuated. There is a curious effect on government consumption in that a large contemporaneous positive coefficient is followed by a coefficient of similar magnitude but opposite sign. The sum of the coefficients is similar to that in the base regressions.

Another specification issue is the inclusion of the country-specific trends. Many of the countries display only limited deviations from stationarity over the sample period, and casual inspection of the data in Figures 1 and 2 suggests that removing the trends may eliminate some of the long-term effects of commodity prices on national output or output growth. When the basic FGLS regressions are reestimated without the country-specific trends, however, the results are similar to those in Table 4, although, once again, there is a larger contemporaneous impact and a slightly attenuated effect on investment.

The choice of deflator for the commodity-price index is less than obvious. For terms-of-trade issues, which have been of much concern in the commodity-price literature, it makes sense to deflate the prices of developing-country commodity exports by the prices of their imports, but the general index used here is not country specific, and even if it were, it might not be the appropriate index for short-term macroeconomic or debt-related issues. One obvious alternative is the U.S. consumer-price index, which differs from the import-price index in a number of respects, the most important of which for the period is the different weighting of petroleum products. Only three Sub-Saharan African countries, Congo, Gabon, and Nigeria, export mainly oil. With the U.S. CPI as deflator, the effects on consumption and investment are reduced and the timing is somewhat altered in the other two equations. When the commodity-price index is restricted to enter with a one-year lag only, the results are similar to those obtained by imposing the same restriction on the baseline data, but with a smaller, although highly significant, effect on investment.

Perhaps the most important data-related issue concerns the national-income accounts. The data from the Penn World Table have several virtues, not the least of which are consistency and a treatment of net exports that should eliminate any direct accounting effect of commodity-price changes on real national output. If there are problems with the PPP corrections that have proportional or even trend effects, they will be eliminated by the country-specific trends and intercepts in our logarithmic specifications. Nonetheless, it seems wise to reexamine the basic results using the standard national-accounts data. The VARX reported in Table 4 was reestimated using the national-output data from the World Bank's *African Economic and Financial Data* (1990), a data source that allows for a slightly longer time span (from 1961 to 1987) than the Penn World Table permits. The results are quite different. In the FGLS regressions, the impact on national output is attenuated, whereas the contemporaneous impact on consumption is negative but is then reversed at one lag. The impact on investment is still positive and large but is more concentrated in the first lag. The impact on government consumption is similar to that on private consumption and is also highly significant. If the commodity-price variable is restricted, however, so that it enters with only a one-year lag, the results are similar to the results when the same restriction is placed on the Penn World Table data. The effects are positive and highly significant in all equations except for private consumption with the World Bank data. Compared with Table 4, the net coefficient is smaller for national output but larger for investment and government expenditure, and the impact on private consumption virtually disappears. The comparison between the two sets of accounts is therefore much more destructive for the detailed dynamics of the effects of commodity prices than it is for the broad conclusions over the medium term, conclusions that will be reinforced when we look at growth rates.

Another specification issue is the assumption of trend stationarity. The obvious alternative is a specification in first differences, and the VARX was estimated in this form including only country-specific intercepts. This leads to a spreading of the impacts more evenly across the lags with greater cumulative elasticities for all four equations. The impact on investment becomes quite large, with a 1 percent permanent increase in the commodity price leading to a cumulative 0.28 percent increase in investment, accounting for only the direct effects. Once again, there are significant positive effects in all the equations. When the alternative national-accounts data are used in place of the Penn World Table data, the results are fairly similar in differences to the corresponding results in levels and are, again, quite different from the Penn World data in both levels and differences. Although the effects on national output and investment remain positive and significant for these data, with greater elasticities than when estimated in levels, the contemporaneous negative effects on government and private consumption that were also found in the levels regressions do not fully reverse, so that the net effect is still negative.

47

We have also reestimated the VARX in Table 4 using "impact weigh-ting," that is, the rescaling of the commodity-price index by the share of the twenty-one commodity exports in GDP in 1975. Impact weighting leads to a similar overall pattern. For national output, investment, and government expenditure, the contemporaneous effect of commodity prices becomes more important. The timing for private consumption is unchanged. Adjusting for the scaling, the coefficients are somewhat smaller, suggesting some nonlinearity in the relationship. For the alternative national-accounts data, the weighting leads to somewhat less significant results (except for investment), although restricting the commodity-price index to enter with only a one-year lag gives similar results to the unweighted regressions.

5 OTHER ISSUES AND VARIATIONS ON THE THEME

In this chapter, we use the data and methodology of Chapter 4 to take up a number of the theoretical issues raised in Chapters 1 and 3. Because the baseline results appear to be inconsistent with at least some of the country evidence, we begin with an examination of the individual country experiences, again looking at the dynamic response of national output to changes in international commodity prices. We then turn to the links between commodity prices and debt and test whether countries that benefited more than most from the commodity-price booms of the 1970s were also the countries that accumulated the most debt. We look at the links between commodity prices and domestic inflation, at the effects of the taxation system on the transmission of fluctuations, at possible asymmetries between booms and slumps, and at differences in the effects of price changes in minerals and nonminerals.

The Experience of Individual Countries

It is not useful to try to replicate the VARX for each country. With a maximum of only twenty-nine annual observations per country, the full VARX with all lags (as in Table 4) would leave us with too few degrees of freedom to give worthwhile results. We must therefore either simplify the VARX, continue to rely on some degree of pooling, or use a different technique. We begin with the last. Figures 6A through 6D show the GDP and commodity-price data for the thirty-two countries. The solid lines in each of the graphs are two alternative estimates of real GDP, one the PPP figure from the Penn World Table, the other the official GDP figure converted at official exchange rates from the World Bank's *African Economic and Financial Data* (1990). Superimposed on the same graphs as a broken line is the country-specific commodity-price index described in Chapter 4. All series are in logarithms and are centered to be zero in 1980.

These graphs raise a number of points for discussion. First, the Penn World Table figures are far from identical to the figures in the IMF's *International Financial Statistics* and the World Bank's *African Economic and Financial Data*. Indeed, they differ by more than would appear to be justified by PPP corrections alone. For Benin, Burundi,

INDICES OF COMMODITY PRICES AND GDP

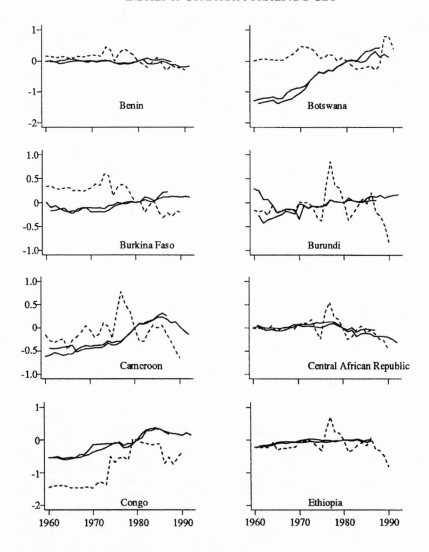

NOTE: Solid lines are estimates of GDP from the World Bank *African Economic and Financial Data* (1990) and Penn World Table (Mark 5.6); broken lines are country-specific commodity-price indices. All indices are converted to logarithms and are centered on zero.

INDICES OF COMMODITY PRICES AND GDP

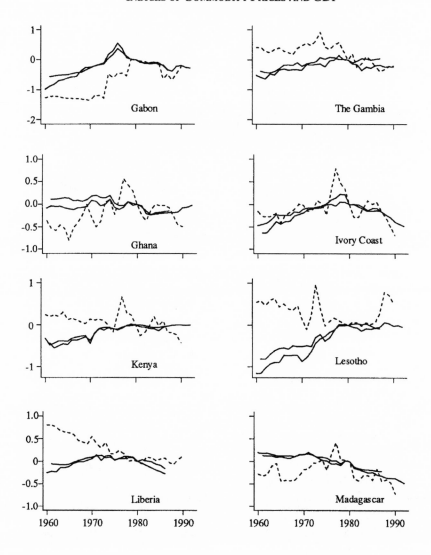

NOTE: Solid lines are estimates of GDP from the World Bank *African Economic and Financial Data* (1990) and Penn World Table (Mark 5.6); broken lines are country-specific commodity-price indices. All indices are converted to logarithms and are centered on zero.

INDICES OF COMMODITY PRICES AND GDP

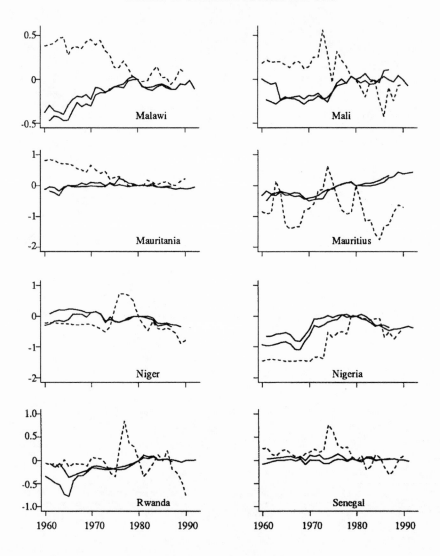

NOTE: Solid lines are estimates of GDP from the World Bank *African Economic and Financial Data* (1990) and Penn World Table (Mark 5.6); broken lines are country-specific commodity-price indices. All indices are converted to logarithms and are centered on zero.

INDICES OF COMMODITY PRICES AND GDP

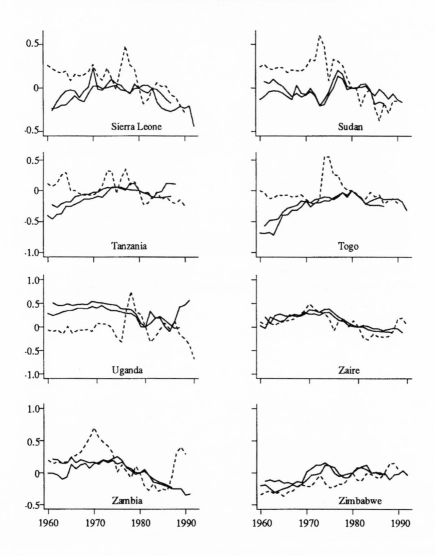

NOTE: Solid lines are estimates of GDP from the World Bank *African Economic and Financial Data* (1990) and Penn World Table (Mark 5.6); broken lines are country-specific commodity-price indices. All indices are converted to logarithms and are centered on zero.

Mauritania, and Senegal, the two series have a correlation coefficient of less than 0.5 in levels, something that is true for half of the countries for the first differences of GDP. Furthermore, the compression of scales in the graphs makes the two estimates of GDP look a good deal closer than they otherwise might. International comparisons of national-accounts data are always hazardous and nowhere more so than in Africa. Even so, the broad pictures of economic growth and decline over three decades are not markedly different for the two series, even if it is risky to rely on the patterns of year-to-year growth rates.

Second, the commodity-price series are shown directly as computed, without any weighting for the importance of exports in each economy. The clearest examples of similarity are provided by the countries that export almost entirely oil—Congo, Gabon, and Nigeria. For these, the commodity-price index is visibly the same. Exports of the twenty-one commodities do not account for the same share of GDP in all the countries, however. It might be argued that the effect of commodity-price changes on GDP is likely to depend, not on the price index directly, but on the price index weighted according to the importance of those exports in the economy. Although we broadly agree with this argument, which was the motivation for the impact-weighted regressions in Chapter 4, it should be noted that there is no law that price must operate in exactly this way. Some of the effects described in the conventional story depend as much on the absolute size of government revenue as on its share of GDP, so that the weighting issue is ultimately an empirical one. For the country-by-country analysis that is the topic of this section, the weighting will simply rescale regression coefficients without affecting fit or significance. From the point of view of the figures, the behavior of the series is more easily seen than when they are weighted by export shares in GDP, which for several countries removes any visible variation in the price.

Figures 6A through 6D confirm the diversity of the individual country experiences. There is certainly no obvious general law whereby GDP is determined by swings in the price of commodity exports. For about half of the countries—Benin, Botswana, Burkina Faso, Kenya, Liberia, Malawi, Mali, Mauritania, Mauritius, Niger, Rwanda, Senegal, Sudan, and Uganda—there is no obvious link between commodity prices and GDP in either the short or long term. Correlations between the two GDP series and the commodity-price index are zero or negative, both in levels and differences. For half of the remaining countries (including the three oil producers)—Central African Republic, Congo, Gabon, Ivory Coast, Madagascar, Nigeria, and Zaire—there appears to be a connection in both the short and the long terms, although the strength of the relationship varies a good deal from country to country. Several other countries—Burundi, Cameroon, and Kenya in the coffee boom, Lesotho in the mid-1970s wool boom, Mauritius in the mid-1970s sugar boom—show some *episodes* during which price changes are closely connected with changes in GDP, but other periods when the relationship does not hold. Finally, there is quite frequently a longer-term relationship. High commodity-price growth in the 1960s and 1970s was associated with much stronger economic performance than was the case in the late 1970s and 1980s, when commodity prices were often declining and growth rates were slower or even negative.

This graphical evidence shows why there is scope for several different interpretations of the experience. Continent-wide relationships, if present, are certainly not strong enough to dominate events, so that we can hardly escape from an econometric analysis that allows us to control for other variables. And although case studies of specific episodes can cast a good deal of light on the political and economic processes that operated during those episodes, it is clearly dangerous to extrapolate the findings, unless they can be shown to apply to all such episodes and to other countries.

One econometric approach to the individual country data is to estimate simplified versions of the VARX, and we have investigated a number of ways of doing this. One way is to regress for each country the logarithm of GDP on its lag, on a time trend, and on one or two lags of the logarithmic commodity-price index. Alternatively, we can experiment with a difference-on-differences approach, in which the growth rate of GDP is regressed on its own lag and on one or two lags of the rate of growth of commodity prices. Given that we have only twenty-nine observations per country, some of which are lost to lagged variables, it is not surprising that many of these regressions fail to yield coefficients that are statistically significantly different from zero. For example, in the levels regression using the Penn World Table data and a single once-lagged commodity-price index, the t-values are absolutely greater than or equal to 1.7 in eight out of thirty-two cases; for an additional four countries, the t-values are greater than or equal to 1.4. All have positive signs. The positive values associated with the large t-values are 0.15 (Botswana), 0.17 (The Gambia), 0.19 (Ghana), 0.05 (Mauritius), 0.14 (Tanzania), 0.23 (Zaire), 0.20 (Zambia), and 0.42 (Zimbabwe). Ignoring t-values, twenty-three of the thirty-two coefficients are positive; the exceptions are Burkina Faso, Congo, Gabon, Lesotho, Mauritania, Nigeria, Sierra Leone, Sudan, and Uganda, a list that includes the three oil producers. The differenced regressions—including the lagged rate of growth of GDP and the lagged rate of growth of commodity prices—differ in detail but are similar in general. There are twenty-two out of thirty-two positive coefficients and four t-values that are greater than 1.5 (for the Central African Republic, Ghana, Liberia, and Mauritania).

These results show the inevitable consequences of trying to make bricks with too little straw; the lack of observations precludes precise estimation and prevents the results from being robust across different specifications and data sets. Although the results confirm the diversity of individual country experience, the broad picture shows why the pan-African VARX yields a positive association between GDP and commodity prices.

One hypothesis suggested by Figures 6A through 6D is that economic growth and commodity prices are linked over longer spans, with GDP and commodity prices linked over quinquennia or decades, rather than over shorter periods. It is impossible to test this contention country by country, because there are only two decades, or four quinquennia, for each. Nevertheless, we can test whether such an association holds over all the countries by pooling the data. The results for different specifications and data sources are shown in Table 5. All the coefficients shown in the table come from regressions of the average annual rate of growth of real GDP over a five-year period on the average annual rate of growth of the commodity-price index over a five-year period. In the top half of the table, we use the GDP data from the Penn World Table, and in the bottom half, we use the World Bank's *African Economic and Financial Data*. Within each half, there are four rows depending on the lag between GDP growth and commodity-price growth. Thus, the first row of the top panel shows a regression in which there are five observations from each country—the growth rates for the quinquennia from 1960, 1965, 1970, 1975, and 1980—and for which GDP and commodity-price growth are contemporaneous. The second row shows four observations per country, the dependent variables being the GDP growth rates for the five-year periods beginning with 1965, 1970, 1975, and 1980, and the independent variable being the commodity-price growth rates for the five years beginning with 1969, 1974, and 1979. The corresponding lags in the third and fourth rows are two and three years, again with four observations from each country. Regressions are run with and without country-specific intercepts, and both sets of results are shown. The regressions have also been rerun with "year" (in this case, quinquennial) dummies, without significant differences in the results.

56

TABLE 5
COMMODITY-PRICE EFFECTS ON GDP: FIVE-YEAR
NONOVERLAPPING GROWTH RATES

	No Weighting		"Impact" Weighting	
	No Dummies	Country Dummies	No Dummies	Country Dummies
Penn World Table Data				
No lag	0.003 (0.1)	−0.005 (0.1)	0.447 (1.9)	0.373 (1.5)
One-year lag	0.085 (1.8)	0.062 (1.2)	0.415 (1.7)	0.289 (1.0)
Two-year lag	0.141 (3.3)	0.135 (3.1)	0.709 (3.1)	0.729 (2.8)
Three-year lag	0.125 (2.9)	0.121 (2.8)	−0.005 (0.0)	−0.299 (1.0)
World Bank Data				
No lag	−0.019 (0.5)	−0.022 (0.5)	0.079 (0.4)	0.046 (0.2)
One-year lag	0.073 (1.6)	0.061 (1.3)	0.198 (1.1)	0.146 (0.8)
Two-year lag	0.124 (2.9)	0.129 (3.1)	0.415 (2.6)	0.450 (2.9)
Three-year lag	0.061 (1.4)	0.062 (1.5)	0.086 (0.5)	0.066 (0.4)

NOTE: In the impact-weighted regressions, the logarithmic commodity-price indices are weighted by the share of the commodity exports in GDP in 1975. Numbers in parentheses are absolute *t*-values.

SOURCES: Penn World Table (Mark 5.6), 1961–1986; World Bank, *African Economic and Financial Data* (1990).

For both types of GDP data, the estimated effects are strongest and most precisely estimated when the lag between the five-year growth rates is at least one year. The inclusion of country dummies tends to reduce somewhat the precision of the estimates and also (in some cases) the estimates themselves, but the effects are small. The right-hand side of the table returns to the issue of weighting commodity-price changes according to the importance of commodity-price exports in GDP. The regressions are run exactly as they are on the left-hand side of the table, but prior to differencing, the logarithm of the commodity-price index is multiplied by the 1975 share in GDP of exports of the twenty-one commodities. By the application of such weights, commodity-price shocks are converted into GDP shocks, or at least their money equivalent. The average over all countries of the export weights is close to 10 percent, so that the estimates on the right-hand side of the table are a good deal larger than those on the left. As before, the inclusion of country dummies has a small effect in reducing both the size and precision of the estimates, but the qualitative conclusions remain the same. An increase in commodity prices that is worth 1 percent of GDP per annum is estimated—over a five-year period—to increase the growth rate of GDP by about half of 1 percent in addition to its direct effects on net income.

These findings do not support the contention that macroeconomic management is so bad in general that increases in commodity prices ultimately decrease either national product or national income. However, they do confirm the perception that the recent relatively poor economic performance of African countries has had something to do with the recent poor performance of the prices of African exports. From 1970 to 1975, the impact-weighted commodity prices grew at 0.27 percent a year for the thirty-two countries as a group while real GDP per capita grew at 2.1 percent a year according to the Penn World Table data and 2.0 percent a year according to the World Bank's *African Economic and Financial Data*. A decade later, from 1980 to 1985, impact-weighted commodity prices *declined* by 0.35 a year, while GDP declined at 1.1 percent a year (Penn World Table) or 0.6 percent a year (World Bank). According to the results in Table 5, about a tenth of this reduction in economic growth rates can be attributed to the reduction in the rate of growth of commodity prices. Commodity prices may not be the only factors that are important for growth in Africa, but they are a part of the story.

Inflation and Debt

Even if commodity-price booms are good for per capita national output, does the experience leave countries "mired in debt and inflation?" This section looks at the evidence.

Table 6 shows the relation between commodity prices and long-term debt; the debt figures come from the World Bank's *World Data* (1994). The definition of long-term debt (defined by the Bank as obligations with maturities greater than one year) is the sum of "debt outstanding" in the categories IBRD, IDA, other multilateral, bilateral, suppliers, commercial banks, bonds, buyers credit, and use of IMF credit. Private nonguaranteed debt is excluded from these figures, an omission that, although possibly large for some of the African countries (Ivory Coast, Kenya, and the oil producers), is necessary to guarantee consistency and quality over all the countries and time periods; indeed, even the official debt figures are only available from 1970, thus shortening the number of observations in these regressions. Each figure in the table is the regression coefficient of the rate of growth of long-term debt over a three-year period on the rate of growth in commodity prices over a

TABLE 6

COMMODITY-PRICE EFFECTS ON LONG-TERM DEBT: THREE-YEAR
NONOVERLAPPING GROWTH RATES

	No Weighting		"Impact" Weighting	
	No Dummies	Country Dummies	No Dummies	Country Dummies
	Penn World Table Data			
No lag	0.004 (0.0)	0.008 (0.1)	−0.258 (0.4)	0.115 (0.1)
One-year lag	−0.182 (1.5)	−0.218 (1.6)	−0.142 (0.2)	0.022 (0.2)
Two-year lag	−0.123 (1.2)	−0.134 (1.2)	−0.517 (0.8)	0.247 (0.2)
Three-year lag	−0.060 (0.7)	−0.071 (0.8)	−0.404 (0.7)	0.212 (0.3)

NOTE: Numbers in parentheses are absolute t-values.
SOURCES: Penn World Table (Mark 5.6), 1961–1986; World Bank, *World Data* (1994).

three-year period. Results are shown for various lags between zero and three; the results for further lags are similar and are not shown. As usual, estimates are presented for impact-weighted commodity prices and for unweighted prices, and as in Table 5, by whether or not country-specific intercepts are included. No matter which way the relationship is estimated, none of the parameters is significantly different from zero. Indeed, to the extent that any pattern is apparent, it is one of negative coefficients, which corresponds to the commonsense finding that commodity-price booms make countries better off and help them reduce their debt. There is no evidence in these estimates, or in those employing longer lags, that commodity-price booms typically leave a legacy of debt.

Because current-account deficits are frequently financed by international borrowing, one way of checking these conclusions is to examine the effect of commodity prices on the current-account balance. The World Bank's *African Economic and Financial Data* provides data on exports and imports in current U.S. dollars. We deflate these by the nominal GDP in U.S. dollars from the same source. Although this is not exactly what we want, it gives some indication of the burden of debt accumulated from the trade balance. If this measure is regressed on its own lags and on the GDP-weighted logarithmic indices of commodity prices, we find a large, positive, and statistically significant contemporaneous effect, followed by a negative coefficient of similar magnitude after one period. Without weighting for the importance of exports in GDP, the sum of these two coefficients is negative, small in absolute value, and significant almost exactly at the 5 percent level. With impact weighting, the pattern is identical but the sum is insignificant. This alternative way of looking at the issue provides no evidence against the previous conclusion, that commodity prices have no long-term effect on debt.

Once again, we emphasize that the results do not disprove that, in individual cases, commodity-price booms were mismanaged to the point of increasing long-term debt. What they do show is that there is no such general result for African countries taken as a group. Indeed, an examination of country-by-country plots of graphs of commodity prices and debt shows that, although there were indeed large increases of debt for the oil, cocoa, and coffee exporters through the late 1970s and early 1980s following the booms in their commodity prices, there were also major increases in debt for countries that experienced no such booms, including the large number of countries with downward trends in the prices of their exports. Although this cannot be taken as evidence that countries with commodity-price booms handled their debt well, they apparently did no worse than other countries. Case studies that reveal an association between debt and commodity prices in the countries with price booms are incomplete unless set against studies of countries without booms but which also increased their debt.

We investigate the role of commodity prices on the general price level using a VARX method, in which the price level and the money supply are the two dependent variables, supplemented by the effects of commodity prices. Table 7 presents the results for the case in which commodity prices are weighted by the average share of commodity exports in GDP. It presents two specifications. The top panel uses logarithmic levels of prices, money, and commodity prices; the bottom panel uses all variables in logarithmic differences. We experimented with two different definitions of domestic prices. The first, shown on the right-hand side of the table, uses the GDP deflator from the World Bank's *African Economic and Financial Data*. Although this is perhaps the obvious measure of prices, it has the disadvantage of containing the automatic effects of changes in world commodity prices. If, as we suspect, the nominal values of GDP count exports of commodities at current world prices converted to local currency, and if constant-price GDP is an output measure, the ratio of the two will by definition increase with increases in the world price of exports. In an attempt to find a price index that is purged of this effect, we constructed and present on the left-hand side of the table a measure of prices from the implicit deflator of *consumption* in the Penn World Table data. The

TABLE 7

COMMODITY-PRICE EFFECTS ON THE GENERAL PRICE LEVEL: EXTENDED VECTOR
AUTOREGRESSIONS (VARX) OF LOGARITHMS OF MONEY AND PRICES

	Penn World Table Consumption Deflator, 1962–1988			AEFD GDP Deflator, 1965–1987		
	Prices		Money	Prices		Money
Specification in Levels						
Prices						
One-year lag	0.787 (18.3)		0.238 (5.6)	0.927 (19.9)		0.290 (4.6)
Two-year lag	0.052 (1.0)		−0.066 (1.3)	−0.183 (3.0)		−0.163 (1.9)
Three-year lag	−0.067 (1.6)		−0.004 (0.1)	0.034 (0.8)		0.011 (0.2)
Money						
One-year lag	0.210 (6.8)		0.894 (21.7)	0.168 (6.6)		0.801 (17.2)
Two-year lag	−0.095 (2.3)		0.001 (0.0)	−0.075 (2.5)		0.039 (0.7)
Three-year lag	0.021 (0.7)		−0.181 (4.3)	0.031 (1.2)		−0.191 (4.0)
Commodity prices						
No lag	0.325 (2.1)		1.076 (6.9)	0.929 (7.7)		1.048 (7.1)
One-year lag	−0.378 (1.9)		−0.278 (1.4)	−0.664 (4.5)		−0.280 (1.5)
Two-year lag	0.140 (0.7)		−0.061 (0.3)	0.029 (0.2)		0.314 (1.5)
Three-year lag	−0.186 (1.1)		−0.181 (1.0)	−0.023 (0.2)		−0.468 (2.6)
Specification in Log Differences						
Inflation						
One-year lag	0.035 (0.8)		0.230 (5.6)	0.215 (4.7)		0.289 (4.7)
Two-year lag	0.109 (2.5)		0.108 (2.5)	0.024 (0.5)		0.038 (0.6)
Three-year lag	0.036 (0.8)		0.081 (1.9)	0.148 (3.3)		0.074 (1.2)
Money growth						
One-year lag	0.197 (6.2)		0.077 (1.8)	0.145 (5.6)		0.019 (0.4)
Two-year lag	0.061 (1.8)		0.076 (1.8)	0.025 (0.9)		0.049 (1.0)
Three-year lag	0.080 (2.4)		0.004 (0.1)	0.031 (1.2)		−0.034 (0.7)
Commodity-price growth						
No lag	0.234 (1.4)		0.994 (6.1)	0.886 (7.3)		1.057 (6.4)
One-year lag	−0.208 (1.2)		0.562 (3.2)	−0.049 (0.4)		0.434 (2.4)
Two-year lag	−0.007 (0.0)		0.405 (2.3)	−0.077 (0.5)		0.598 (3.0)
Three-year lag	−0.149 (0.8)		−0.088 (0.5)	−0.187 (1.4)		−0.189 (1.0)

NOTE: Figures are impact-weighted by the average share of exports of the twenty commodities in GDP. They exclude Liberia, for which no money-supply data are available, Lesotho for most years, Kenya and Tanzania for 1975, Zimbabwe before 1975, and Botswana before 1976. The construction of the Penn World Table consumption deflator is explained in the text. The AEFD GDP deflator is taken from the World Bank's *African Economic and Financial Data*. Numbers in parentheses are absolute *t*-values.

SOURCES: Penn World Table (Mark 5.6); World Bank, *African Economic and Financial Data* (1990).

ratio of current to real consumption from the Penn World Table, which is a PPP index expressed as a fraction of the U.S. dollar exchange rate, is multiplied first by the exchange rate, to convert it to local currency, and then by the ratio of current to constant-price GDP in U.S. dollars, to pick up the amount by which prices have increased since the base year. In Table 7, where it appears on the left-hand side, it is called the Penn World Table consumption deflator. In all cases, the VARX includes country-specific intercepts and time trends.

The major differences between the top and bottom of the table are, as is to be expected, on the "own" first lags, with the differencing eliminating much of the autocorrelation in the levels. The difference between the two price measures is that commodity prices (or the growth of commodity prices) has a large and significant instantaneous effect on the GDP deflator but very little effect on the Penn World Table consumption deflator. We take this as an indication that the construction of the latter has successfully removed the accounting effect of commodity prices in the price indices. Apart from this, the main influence of commodity-price changes on inflation comes, not directly, but through current and lagged effects on money, which is significantly positive in all four price regressions, in levels, in differences, and using both deflators. The impulse-response functions for the price level and for inflation are shown in Figure 7. The top part of the figure shows that, in a country where 25 percent of GDP comes from commodity exports, a 10 percent increase in world prices would raise the GDP deflator by 2.5 percent in the first year but would raise the consumption deflator by only 0.5 percent in the first year and by a little over 1 percent in the subsequent four years. The bottom part of the figure shows the same price increase in terms of the additional inflation introduced into the system.

The effects shown in the figure are qualitatively what would be predicted by either Dutch-disease or construction-boom theory. The increase in domestic incomes raises the relative price of nontradables, so that there will be an increase in domestic prices unless there is a compensating monetary contraction. Some limited experiments to check whether the price increases are larger for the investment deflator than for the consumption deflator were also run. Construction-boom theory predicts that, in the presence of controls on imports and investment abroad, the additional saving generated by windfall incomes from commodity booms is diverted into domestic investment, stimulating both output and the relative prices of nontraded investment goods. VARX regressions including the investment deflator, however, show effects that

62

FIGURE 7

IMPULSE RESPONSE OF PRICES AND INFLATION TO COMMODITY PRICES

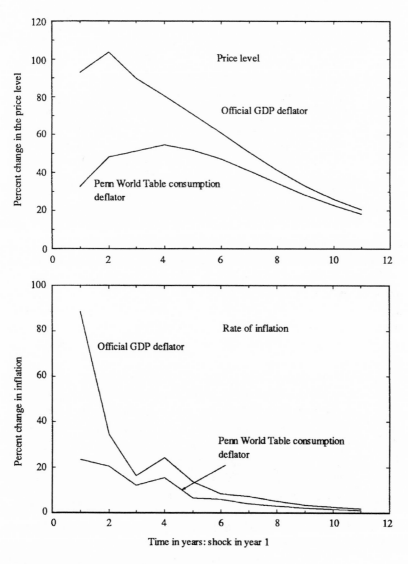

SOURCE: Authors' calculations as described in the text.

are very similar to those for the consumption deflator shown in Figure 7. We could find no evidence that commodity-price increases raise the price of investment relative to consumption. It is not possible using these data to examine the relative price of nontradable investment goods.

Asymmetry, Minerals and Taxation

In this section, we run a number of alternative sets of regressions to investigate hypotheses suggested by the literature reviewed in Chapter 3. One possible hypothesis is that the responses to commodity booms are different from the responses to slumps. Governments may be only too willing to embark on investment programs in response to windfall gains, but they find it difficult to cut expenditures when prices fall. As a result, the expansion during the boom may favor low-quality projects, whereas the cuts during the slump fall on productive government services. We started from the VARX in differences as discussed in Chapter 4 and reestimated with price increases and decreases entered separately and with the coefficients allowed to differ. The results show little evidence of asymmetry. There is a weak tendency for upswings to have a greater impact on investment, but it is, at best, only marginally significant. For the other equations, the direction is also toward more impact for booms, but the difference is small and insignificant. This finding makes it clear that the baseline results using the linear (symmetric) model were not caused by booms that had no positive effects or slumps that had strong negative effects.

Another issue is whether mineral prices and nonmineral prices have the same effects. Again, there are reasons for suspecting not. Minerals are typically produced in enclaves, often by very few employees (see Gersovitz and Paxson, 1990, for estimates), and in almost all cases, they are essentially owned by the government. It is hard to tax smallholder agriculture at close to 100 percent, if only because of the possibility of smuggling, something that is not an issue for minerals other than diamonds. Mineral-price booms therefore do not generate the widespread income increases among smallholders that follow agricultural price increases in countries where the procurement price moves at least partly with the world price. We estimated mineral and nonmineral price indices using the same principles as for the general export-price index. In some cases, where countries export no minerals, the price index is set to zero; although this is arbitrary, it has no effect in the presence of country-specific intercepts. The results assign considerably greater effects to the nonmineral prices. Prices of minerals, including oil, show relatively little effect on output, and although there is some

64

evidence of an effect of mineral prices on investment, there is none for any of the other components of national output. This result is important, not just because it confirms the distinction between enclave and farmer commodities, but because it challenges the supposition that governments always spend the windfall proceeds of export taxes. If governments willingly spend, or by political pressures are forced to spend, all discretionary income, there is no reason for any difference between revenues from minerals and those from agricultural goods. Indeed, some of the most egregious examples of misspending come from Nigeria's response to windfall oil incomes. The finding suggests, rather, that the original results depend on the private sector's receiving at least some of the windfall and holds out hope that the investment effects in Table 4 and Figure 5 come at least in part from the private sector.

TABLE 8

COUNTRIES IN THE VECTOR AUTOREGRESSION (VAR) AND CLASSIFICATION BY COMMODITY-TAX REGIME

Country	High Price	Floater	Country	High Price	Floater
Benin	0	0	Malawi	0	0
Botswana	—	—	Mali	0	0
Burkina Faso	0	0	Mauritania	—	—
Burundi	1	1	Mauritius	—	—
Cameroon	1	1	Niger	1	0
C.A.R	0	1	Nigeria	1	0
Congo	0	1	Rwanda	1	0
Ethiopia	1	0	Senegal	1	0
Gabon	—	—	Sierra Leone	1	1
The Gambia	1	0	Sudan	1	—
Ghana	0	0	Tanzania	1	0
Ivory Coast	1	0	Togo	0	0
Kenya	1	0	Uganda	0	0
Lesotho	—	—	Zaire	0	0
Liberia	1	1	Zambia	0	0
Madagascar	1	1	Zimbabwe	1	1

NOTE: "High price" is based on the producers' share of the world price of the most important agricultural export commodities and takes the value of 1 for countries with low taxes (high prices) and zero for countries with high taxes (low prices.) "Floater" is 1 for countries where the producer price is highly correlated with the world price and is 0 otherwise. Procurement prices in local currency are taken from the World Bank's *World Data* (1994) and converted to U.S. dollars using the PPP exchange rates implicit in the Penn World Table. Ratios and correlations are then calculated using world prices in U.S. dollars. Direct estimates of ratios of producer price to world prices are given by the World Bank, *African Economic and Financial Data* (1990), but these appear to be based on official exchange rates and lead to many obvious misclassifications.

Finally, there is the question of whether tax systems matter, whether the rate of tax itself has an effect on stabilization policy and whether the way in which windfalls are shared between public and private sectors is significant. If it is, the responses of GDP and its components to commodity-price fluctuations will vary from country to country, so that pooled VARs will be misspecified and possibly misleading, even for the continent as a whole. Country differences might also explain the discordance between the generally negative descriptions in the literature and the lack of any obvious negative effects in the econometric results. To address these questions, we carried out crude tests of the effects of tax systems by splitting countries into two groups according to two different criteria. In the first split, the ratio of producer prices to world prices was used to split countries into high or low taxers, with some countries unassigned because of data problems. The second split was based on the correlation between producer prices and world prices, so that countries were sorted, where possible, into "floaters" and "nonfloaters." The results of the assignment are shown in Table 8 (on page 65). Perhaps surprisingly, the results of the VAR do not differ significantly across either of the two splits. Given the importance of this issue for questions on taxation and public expenditure (see Chapter 3), a good deal more investigation is warranted.

6 THE PRICE OF POWER:
FROM COMMODITY PRICES TO POLITICS

In this final chapter, we step back from the economic impacts of commodity-price fluctuations and turn to political impacts and the relation between political change and economic growth. We do this in part simply to broaden our enquiry into the effects of world price fluctuations. More fundamentally, however, because political and economic events in an individual country usually have little effect on world commodity prices, and because those world prices have a demonstrable effect on the growth rate of national output, we can use the fluctuations in commodity prices as an instrument to help understand the interaction between political and economic events.

There are two different literatures that address the relation between political factors and economic growth. One, in economics, looks at the determinants of economic growth; the other, in political science, considers the determinants of political structure and political change. The literature on economic growth, although mostly concerned with economic determinants, often includes a number of political variables such as the level of political or civil freedom, the extent to which the political system is democratic, and measures of political instability such as political violence or frequent or irregular changes of regime. The political-science literature, often working with much the same data, looks for the economic determinants of political structures and asks whether democracy is a luxury good, whether irregular transfers of power are confined to poor countries, and whether and to what extent transfers of power are inhibited by successful economic performance.

Although the empirical evidence shows clear correlations between economic and political variables, it reveals little about the directions of causality. A few studies have attempted to sort out cause and effect but with little success. This is unfortunate, because it is hard to imagine an empirical issue with greater implications for policy. If economic performance is the inevitable precursor of political change, economic growth in East Asia will lead to political liberalization, and international policy should be directed toward encouraging that growth, leaving political structures to look after themselves. Similarly, the key to growth and democracy in Africa will be economic reform, not direct political reform. If causality flows in the other direction, however, there will be little hope for economic progress in Africa until political structures are addressed. That will require of the international community a quite different set of policies, policies that might well inhibit or delay economic growth. Of course, the world may not be so simple, and causality may flow in both directions (the incumbent who stimulates the economy prior to an election presumably does so in the belief that economic growth will help him), and it may run in different directions in different times and circumstances.

Using the evidence to establish the direction of causality is hampered by both theoretical and empirical obstacles. Causality is not easily investigated without an agreed upon and empirically tested theoretical structure, in this case of the determinants of economic growth. In spite of the recent revival of interest in the topic, or perhaps because of it, such a structure seems more elusive than ever. The problem is not a lack of theory, but a multiplicity of theories, none of which seems to explain more than a fraction of the historical and geographical variation in growth rates or appears to have any decisive empirical advantage over the others. No current theory provides precisely what we need to test causality, that is, a variable or set of variables that either determines economic outcomes but is uninfluenced by political structure or determines political events but is unaffected by economics. If x affects the growth rate of national income, for example, but is plausibly unaffected by domestic political events, x should help to predict the politics if economics causes politics but should be uncorrelated with political events if causation flows from politics to economics. Commodity prices are an obvious candidate for the instrument x. They are typically set in world markets, to which African producers contribute only a share, and they are thus not likely to be affected by political events in African countries. Increases in commodity prices increase producers' incomes, not only through the direct effects of higher prices, but also by stimulating government expenditure and domestic investment and, through a multiplier-accelerator process, GDP. Fluctuations in world prices thus fulfil the conditions for an instrument; they are exogenous to the domestic political process, and they help predict economic outcomes.

Our discussion is laid out as follows. We first review some previous literature and use it to explain why causality is so difficult to test and why previous attempts have been unconvincing. We then establish a baseline for the experiments. We present the data on leadership, commodity prices, and economic growth and reestablish on our data the earlier results in the literature on economic growth and political survival.

We then test the link between fluctuations in commodity prices and the survival of leaders and present instrumental-variable (IV) estimates.

The results require careful interpretation. They confirm the difficulty of testing causality; commodity prices affect economic growth, and economic growth affects leadership, but neither of the links is individually strong enough to prevent the effect of commodity prices on political events from being quite attenuated. Even so, the results provide no evidence of the feedback from leadership changes to economic growth that would call for a reevaluation of the main result that economic growth inhibits the political exit of leaders. These results are strengthened and reinforced if we admit a wider range of instruments, particularly the lags of those components of national income that are known to predict income change. In all cases, the causality appears to run from the economic to the political events.

Our evidence concerns only one type of political event, political exit, and considers only one economic variable, the rate of economic growth. Its contribution to the broad questions is therefore modest and is made more so by the ambiguity of a good deal of the evidence. Untangling causality is genuinely difficult, however, and the results should be treated as a first step in that process.

Economic and Political Interactions: Some Recent Literature

A large recent empirical literature in economics examines the correlates of economic growth, typically using the international national-income data from the Penn World Table merged with a range of other data on political, social, and economic variables. Most of these studies use averaged growth rates from 1960 to 1985 and treat each country as a separate, single observation. Several have investigated the effects of various measures of democracy on growth, including, for example, the Gastil (1987, Freedom House) measures of civil and political liberties. The results are mixed. Kormendi and Meguire (1985), Scully (1988, 1992), Grier and Tullock (1989), Dasgupta and Weale (1992), and Dasgupta (1993) all find a positive effect of democracy on growth. Sirowy and Inkeles (1990) review a dozen more studies that either show negative or no effects. Helliwell (1992), who also provides a review of the literature, finds no effect of democracy on growth when democracy is added to the predictors in the education-augmented version of the Solow growth model proposed and estimated by Mankiw, Romer, and Weil (1992). Barro (1991a, 1991b) regresses growth rates on, *inter alia*, measures of political instability (including war, assassinations, and revolutions), dummies for socialist versus mixed and capitalist systems, and the Gastil measure of political liberties and finds that all of them, in one specification or another, reduce the rate of economic growth.

To the extent that these studies concern themselves with simultaneity—and several do not—the main "treatment" is timing, with attempts whenever possible to date the political observations earlier than the growth that they are intended to explain. This is not always possible; for example, the Gastil indices are only available from 1976, a problem that Helliwell deals with by instrumentation using all the economic variables in the growth model and the 1960 value of Bollen's (1980) index, with which the 1976 value of the Gastil index is positively correlated. It is important to note that the identification of causality by timing, the *post hoc ergo propter hoc* method, is far from uncontroversial. In particular, political events often cause economic changes that occur *before* the political events themselves; the political business cycle in industrial countries is the classic case in which incumbents attempt to manipulate the economy in anticipation of a forthcoming election.

Nor are revolutions, coups, and political violence random and causeless events; they are often the result of conditions that may themselves have had a prior and long-standing positive (for example, Iran of Pahlavi) or negative (for example, the USSR) effect on economic growth. More generally, whenever there are country-specific "fixed effects," factors that vary from country to country but that are either constant or that change only slowly over time, there will be a feedback from lagged variables to current variables. If some countries are blessed with traditions of entrepreneurship and hard work and some are not, the former will grow faster than the average whatever other factors are at work. Thus, if there is positive feedback from economic growth to political stability in the same period (say), economic growth will be positively predicted by political stability in all earlier periods. In the presence of simultaneity at *any* lag, the omission of any constant or slowly changing variable will affect apparent causality at *all* leads and lags. Thus, unless we can be sure that all such variables have been accounted for, an assurance that is hard to come by, it is not possible to resolve causality questions by timing alone.

Helliwell's instrumentation procedure is exactly the right technique but is nevertheless always likely to be controversial in practice. It is certainly correct that the effects of democracy should be tested within a well-specified model of economic growth, and Mankiw, Romer, and Weil (1992) provide such a model. But the identification of that model is itself extremely controversial; for example, expenditure on schooling

70

appears as an exogenous variable to explain the rate of growth of national output, a specification that is not obviously preferable to the older "demand-for-education" models that assume the opposite causality. A well-specified model is of relatively little help if its own identification is inherently controversial.

Just as economists tend to treat political variables as exogenous, political scientists frequently treat economic variables as exogenous. There is a long-standing literature in political science that considers whether democracy is a "luxury good," something that can be afforded only by relatively rich countries. These studies (reviewed by Helliwell, 1992), tend to endorse the view that democracy is bad for growth. They are typically supported, however, by evidence that rich countries are indeed more democratic, a correlation that, according to Helliwell, is quite robust. There is also strong evidence from Londregan and Poole (1990) that "irregular transfers of powers," or *coups d'état*, are characteristic of poor countries and are almost unknown in the industrial world.

A recent literature in political science (Bienen and van de Walle, 1991, 1992; Bienen, Londregan, and van de Walle, 1993) investigates transfers of power from one leader to the next. It is this work that provides the starting point for our investigations. Bienen and van de Walle link the (conditional) probability of a leader's survival to his or her age, to time in power, and to whether or not the leader assumed power constitutionally. In Bienen, Londregan, and van de Walle, the leader-based analysis, in which each leader is a single observation, is extended to an analysis based on time-series cross-sectional country data, in which each observation is for a given country in a given year, thus allowing an investigation of the role of ethnicity and of economic factors. The study finds that current and lagged economic growth inhibit the transfer of power, so that leaders who are apparently successful in handling the economy or are otherwise economically fortunate are more likely to survive. This result is in line with the literature on democracies in the industrial world. The authors recognize the possible simultaneity between transfers of power and the *current* rate of economic growth and instrument the latter using lagged national income, a measure of openness to trade, and a world business-cycle variable that is weighted by openness to trade. As always, the exogeneity of these instruments is controversial, as is the use of lags to generate exogenous instruments.

Bienen's and Londregan's causality, from economic growth to political survival, is the same as that in Londregan and Poole (1990), who look only at *coups d'état*. Londregan and Poole construct a two-equation model of *coups* and growth and directly confront the simultaneity

71

issue, recognizing that their model cannot be identified without explicit assumptions. On the assumption that there is no instantaneous relationship either from income growth to the probability of a *coup* or from the probability of a *coup* to the current rate of income growth, and that the past history of *coups* has no effect on income, they estimate a model in which income growth is estimated to inhibit *coups d'état*. Because the model contains more identifying assumptions than are strictly necessary, the overidentification can be tested. The results give no indication of misspecification. Even so, the identification itself cannot be tested, and Londregan's and Poole's results are conditional on the validity of their assumptions, which impose a causal structure on the correlations.

Closely related to the literature on political turnover is a set of three recent papers that are concerned with the economic effects of political instability, defined as the probability of a change of leadership (Özler and Tabellini, 1991; Alesina et al., 1992; Cukierman, Edwards, and Tabellini, 1992). All of these papers recognize potential simultaneity between political instability and economic variables, and all use a two-stage procedure that models the probability of a transfer of power at the first stage and then uses the estimated probability of change as a measure of political instability in the subsequent analysis. Cukierman, Edwards, and Tabellini look at the effects of political instability on public finance, particularly on the propensity to finance government by seigniorage. Özler and Tabellini ask whether political instability induces myopia and thus increases the demand for debt by developing countries, and Alesina et al. follow Londregan and Poole in estimating a full-fledged simultaneous model of growth and political change. Their first-stage estimation probability of change uses all of the exogenous variables and, as in the rest of the literature, treats lagged economic and political variables as exogenous (Alesina et al., 1992).

In their simultaneous-equations model, Alesina et al. choose not to follow Londregan and Poole in explicitly justifying their identifying assumptions but to use instead the unusual procedure of excluding exogenous variables based on their insignificance in the reduced form. The standard exclusion methodology of simultaneous-equation estimation requires that variables be excluded *a priori* from the structural equations but not from the reduced form, and absence from the former is no guarantee of absence from the latter. In addition, identification cannot be achieved by the exclusion of irrelevant variables; indeed, it is the prior exclusion of *significant* variables from one or other of the equations that identifies the structure. From the point of view of the current study, the major finding of Alesina et al. is that, in the simultaneous-equation model, neither current nor lagged economic growth has any effect on the probability of a transfer of power. It is tempting to attribute this result to the failure of identification, particularly because the authors' final structural equation for power change has no role whatever—current or lagged, direct or indirect—for economic growth in affecting the transfer of power. The result contradicts not only the rest of the literature, but seemingly also their own reduced-form estimates, in which lagged growth has an important and statistically significant inhibiting effect on political exit.

Lest this section end on an unduly negative tone, we should empha-size the basic intractability of the identification issue that all of these authors have had to address. In the absence of some influence from outside the political and economic system of each country, these political economy models remain essentially unidentified; the best they can do is to demonstrate that it is possible to use the data to tell one story or another. Using the political variables to explain the progress of the economy is just as valid as explaining the political situation by the economic variables. The papers discussed in this section have made major contributions by providing alternative models of the relation between political and economic events and by showing how to interpret the correlations in the data in terms of these models. What none has managed to do is to demonstrate which interpretation is correct.

Establishing the Baseline: Political Exit and Economic Growth

In this section, we use data from Africa to reestablish the same sort of single-equation results for the relation between political exit and economic growth that were earlier obtained for a wider sample by Bienen, Londregan, and van de Walle (1993). Our results are designed to complement the link, documented in Chapter 4, between commodity-price fluctuations and national output. In the next section, we combine the two sets of results into a model of political change that expressly accounts for simultaneity.

Our data on political change come from the compilation of world leaders by Bienen and van de Walle (1991, appendix) covering 2,256 leaders. The data set includes information on the number of years in power, the date of entry to power, whether the leader came to power constitutionally or nonconstitutionally, the leader's age at entry, and whether the exit from power was constitutional, nonconstitutional, or by death from natural causes. As subsequently updated by Bienen,

73

Londregan, and van de Walle (1993), there are forty-four African countries in the compilation, with observations running from 1962 (or from the date of independence, whichever is later) to 1989. In our study, as in theirs, the data are converted so that each observation relates to a specific country in a specific year, rather than to a particular leader. Although the data will be further curtailed to match the availability of national-income and commodity-price data, we have in principle up to twenty-eight observations for each of forty-four countries. From these, we use a dummy variable that takes the value 1 if the country experiences a "political exit" caused by any reason other than death from natural causes. Multiple exits in a single year are treated as if they were a single exit. In order to capture the main results from Bienen and van de Walle, we also use data on the length of time the leader has been in power and on whether that leader's entry was or was not constitutional.

We use the same Penn World Table data on national income and output as in the rest of our study. Replacing these figures with those from the World Bank's *African Economic and Financial Data* has no material effect on the results of the analysis. In order to maximize our chances of significant findings, we include data on all of Africa, including countries north of the Sahara. We thus have thirty-seven countries—all of which are included in the Bienen and van de Walle data—for the years 1965 through 1985.

Bienen and van de Walle (1991) specify the conditional probability of losing power through the hazard function and employ survival analysis to estimate the parameters of their model. Londregan and Poole (1990), in their study of *coups d'état*, use probit analysis, an alternative to survival analysis for handling binary dependent variables. In this study, we follow Bienen, Londregan, and van de Walle (1993) and use the linear-probability model, which essentially ignores the dichotomous structure of the dependent variables and applies standard regression methods. The predictions of the linear-probability model can be interpreted as the probability of an exit, and its coefficients as the effects of the explanatory variables on that probability. The standard regression structure also makes possible the use of fixed-effect estimators, which allow the intercept of the regression to differ from country to country. Given the timing and exogeneity issues discussed in the previous section, it is important to be able to allow for such effects even if, in some cases, the relevant results can only be identified from the cross-country variation in the data. Clearly, the functional form of the linear-probability model is less satisfactory than one guaranteeing that probabilities lie between 1 and zero. The problem seems hardly decisive in an exercise such as this, however, where the model is not tightly specified and where we are concerned with little more than detecting correlations, measuring their significance, and interpreting them within a causal framework.

The linear-probability results for leader exit are given in Table 9. The right- and left-hand sides of the table show results with and without country-specific intercepts, and each half shows results for a specification containing only the growth rate of real output and for a specification containing growth, time in power, the nonconstitutional-entry dummy, and an interaction term between the last two. The timing of the growth rate in Table 9 is contemporaneous with the possible exit; the table compares an exit or no exit in year t with the growth of real national output from $t - 1$ to t. The results are consistent with those obtained by Bienen and van de Walle (1991) and by Bienen, Londregan, and van de Walle (1993). There is a strongly significant negative relation between the current rate of economic growth and the probability of exit; in the simplest regression, raising the growth rate from zero to 5 percent a year reduces the predicted probability of exit by 2.5 percent. The effect is somewhat less in the regressions with country fixed effects, but its significance survives the addition of the thirty-six additional explanatory variables. The estimated growth effect is essentially unaffected by the inclusion of the variables relating to the leader currently in power. In the model without fixed effects, we find, as did Bienen and van de Walle, that nonconstitutional leaders are more likely to exit in the early years, but that the effect wears off with time, so that after eight years, a leader who came to power nonconstitutionally is no more likely to exit than one whose entrance was made in the recommended manner. The precise size of these effects should not be taken too seriously, given the crudeness of the specification, but the result accords exactly with the findings of Bienen and van de Walle for a much larger sample of leaders. What is not consistent with their findings is the fact that time in power seems not to enhance the probability of exit in these African countries, except for leaders whose entrance was nonconstitutional. In Africa, many of the constitutional leaders are the first leaders of their new nations, and their tenure is likely to be different from that of leaders elsewhere.

The estimates of the effects of the leadership variables are very similar whether or not fixed effects are included, although none is significantly different from zero in the expanded specification. Even so, the fact that the parameters do not change by much is itself important

TABLE 9

LEADERSHIP-SURVIVAL REGRESSIONS FOR THIRTY-SEVEN AFRICAN COUNTRIES,
1965–1985

	Without Fixed Effects		With Country Fixed Effects	
GDP growth	−0.5128 (3.6)	−0.5207 (3.6)	−0.4216 (2.8)	−0.4459 (3.0)
Time in power		−0.0011 (0.7)		−0.0064 (1.4)
Nonconstitutional entry		0.0685 (2.1)		−0.0606 (1.4)
Time X nonconst. entry		−0.0088 (2.2)		−0.0064 (1.4)
R^2	0.0184	0.0322	0.1121	0.1234

NOTE: The dependent variable refers to an exit in country i in year t; GDP growth refers to the change in the logarithm of GDP from $t - 1$ to t. Estimation is by OLS, with and without the inclusion of dummies for each of the thirty-seven countries. The dependent variable is 1 if leader makes a political exit and is 0 otherwise. Numbers in parentheses are absolute t-values.

in the light of possible causal feedbacks that might be exposed by the inclusion of the fixed effects. There is no evidence in Table 9 that the pooled estimates on the left-hand side of the table are generated by the existence of country-specific effects that are conducive to both political stability and economic growth.

Several possible variants of these results are worth considering. In particular, it is possible that the growth of national output acts as a proxy for other variables that have a more direct impact on the probability of political survival. For example, it is consumption, not national output, that most directly contributes to constituents' welfare; an increase in output that reflects an increase in investment for the future might not be as popular as a direct increase in consumption. It is also true that it is government expenditure that is most directly under the control of the incumbent, so an argument can also be made for the use of government expenditure in place of or in addition to national output. We reran the regressions in Table 9 with the growth of income replaced, in turn, by the growth of investment, consumption, and government expenditure. In all cases, the coefficients were negative and either statistically significant or close to significant, although they were all smaller—between −0.1 and −0.2—than the coefficients on the growth of national output in Table 9. None of these equations fits as well as the original, and none of the alternative variables attracts a t-value as large as those in Table 9.

We also investigated the use of the growth rates of consumption, investment, and government expenditure in addition to the growth rate of national output. In the regressions without fixed effects, the growth rate of output always remains negative and significant, although the effect is somewhat smaller than in Table 9, and it is never possible to reject the hypothesis that the additional variable is irrelevant once we have allowed for output growth. When country fixed effects are included, t-values are further reduced, although the growth rate of income continues to have a negative effect that both is larger and attracts a larger t-value than the additional components of output growth. On the basis of these results, we conclude that output growth performs better than the obvious alternatives and that there is no evidence of additional explanatory power once overall growth has been taken into account.

The other extension investigated in this study is the presence of lagged growth rates. Table 10 presents the results of rerunning the basic regressions including the first and second lags of GDP growth. As with the current growth rate, the estimated effects of lagged growth rates are negative, inhibiting political exit. In none of the four regressions, however, is it possible to reject the hypothesis that, once current growth has been accounted for, earlier lags have no effect. The coefficient on current GDP growth is not much affected by the presence or absence of the lags. Given these results, it is not surprising that there is also little improvement in these regressions from adding lagged values of the growth rates of other components of GDP. In a regression with current and once-lagged values of the growth rates of GDP, consumption, investment, and government expenditure, no single parameter estimate is statistically significant. Once again, it is not possible to reject the hypothesis that only current growth matters.

TABLE 10

LEADERSHIP AND GROWTH OF GDP IN THIRTY-SEVEN AFRICAN
COUNTRIES, 1967–1985

	Without Fixed Effects		With Country Fixed Effects	
GDP growth	−0.4534 (3.1)	−0.4152 (2.8)	−0.4050 (2.7)	−0.3998 (2.6)
Lagged once	−0.2130 (1.5)	−0.1686 (1.1)	−0.1792 (1.2)	−0.1613 (1.1)
Lagged twice		0.02302 (1.5)		−0.2179 (1.4)
		$F(6,619) = 1.41$		$F(6,585) = 1.34$

NOTE: The dependent variable refers to an exit in country i in year t; GDP growth refers to the change in the logarithm of GDP from $t - 1$ to t. Estimation is by OLS, with and without the inclusion of dummies for each of the thirty-seven countries. The dependent variable is 1 if leader makes a political exit and is 0 otherwise. Numbers in parentheses are absolute t-values.

77

Political exit in Africa appears to be retarded by high rates of economic growth, and high rates of economic growth are helped by commodity-price booms. What, then, is the relation between commodity prices and political exit, and can we use commodity prices, which plausibly are determined outside the domestic economy, as an instrument to determine whether the direction of causality is from economic growth to political exit, or from political exit to economic growth? If commodity-price growth makes African economies grow more rapidly, and if more rapid growth retards the turnover of leaders, we ought to be able to observe a direct link between commodity-price change and political exit.

Figures 8 and 9 plot the two variables and the relation between them. Figure 8 shows the average growth rate over all the African countries of the real commodity-price series; because the series are weighted by the share of commodity exports in GDP in 1975, the scale can be interpreted as showing the equivalent increase or decrease in national income associated with the change in prices. From the late 1960s through the early 1970s, the prices of these primary-commodity exports were generally rising in real terms; at the peak in 1973, the African countries exporting these commodities received, on average, the equivalent of about 2.5 percent of national income in price increases. The late 1970s showed considerable volatility in the growth rate, but since 1980, real prices have generally been falling. The growth rates in Figure 8 are averaged over all the commodities listed in Table 3, and the volatility reflects not only the volatility of each commodity price, but also the fact that the commodity prices are far from being perfectly correlated and that different countries export different commodities.

Figure 9 shows the rate of political exit (or the empirical probability of exit) averaged over countries and years according to the rate of real commodity-price growth. There are 818 country-year observations, once missing observations are dropped, and these are gathered into ten groups of eighty-two (or eighty-one) according to the price growth. Each bar in Figure 9 thus corresponds to a decile of commodity-price growth, with negative growth to the left and positive growth to the right. With some imagination, it is possible to see a negative correlation here, but it is clearly extremely weak.

Table 11 shows that the weakness of the relationship is replicated in more formal analyses. With or without country fixed effects, the pooled cross-country time-series regressions of exit on price growth fail to show significant results. Although the coefficients are negative on the

78

FIGURE 8

INCOME FROM COMMODITY-PRICE GROWTH

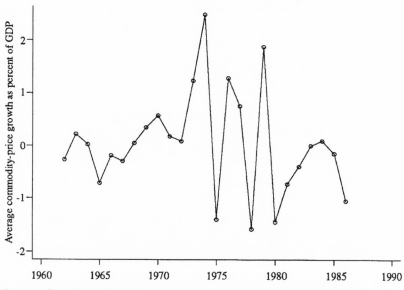

SOURCES: Penn World Table (Mark 5.6) and constructed commodity-price indices.

FIGURE 9

POLITICAL EXIT AND COMMODITY-PRICE GROWTH

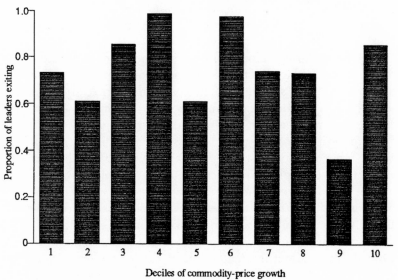

SOURCE: Authors' calculations.

TABLE 11
COMMODITY-PRICE GROWTH AND POLITICAL EXIT IN THIRTY-SEVEN AFRICAN COUNTRIES, 1967–1985

	Without Fixed Effects		With Country Fixed Effects	
$\Delta \ln p_t$	−0.0860 (0.3)	−0.1178 (0.4)	−0.0693 (0.2)	−0.1048 (0.4)
$\Delta \ln p_{t-1}$		−0.3580 (1.1)		−0.3780 (1.2)
$\Delta \ln p_{t-2}$		0.1624 (0.5)		0.1502 (0.5)

NOTE: The dependent variable refers to an exit in country i in year t. Estimation is by OLS, with and without the inclusion of dummies for each of the thirty-seven countries. The dependent variable is 1 if leader makes a political exit and is 0 otherwise. Numbers in parentheses are absolute t-values.

contemporaneous and first lags and on the sum of the lags, for none of these regressions is it possible to reject the hypothesis that political exit is unaffected by changes in commodity prices. It is important to note, however, that although these weak results can hardly be taken as support for the basic hypothesis, they cast no doubt on it. In Table 9, the coefficient of GDP growth on the probability of exit is −0.5. Table 12, which is the first-differenced version of (part of) Table 4 and which shows the first-stage regressions of the growth rate of GDP on commodity prices, gives a coefficient of commodity-price growth on GDP of 0.4; by substitution, then, the effect of commodity-price growth on the probability of exit ought to be −0.2, as opposed to −0.1 in Table 11. And although the coefficients in Tables 9 and 12 are both significant, both regressions have low explanatory power, which will be further attenuated in the regression of exit on prices. We shall return to this issue in the context of the IV estimates below.

If the growth in commodity prices is to be used as an instrumental variable to study the effect of economic growth on political exit, two conditions must be satisfied. First, commodity-price growth must be unaffected by political exit, and second, commodity-price growth should affect political exit only indirectly, through its effect on the growth of output. Although it is possible to think of exceptions—a strike or other political instability in Zaire might affect the world price of copper, for example—the first condition will hold for most of these countries (see Gersovitz and Paxson, 1990, for a discussion of the general issue). For most of the commodities used to construct the indices, African countries are price takers, and even in those cases in which individual countries have a large share of the market, they have limited ability to affect the market price. The second condition is more

TABLE 12

COMMODITY PRICES AND GROWTH OF GDP IN THIRTY-SEVEN AFRICAN COUNTRIES, 1967–1985

	Without Fixed Effects				With Country Fixed Effects			
$\Delta\ln p_t$	0.3970 (4.8)	0.4045 (4.9)	0.4169 (5.1)	0.4228 (5.3)	0.3518 (4.3)	0.3677 (4.4)	0.3682 (4.4)	0.3733 (4.5)
$\Delta\ln p_{t-1}$		0.0521 (0.6)	0.0131 (0.2)	0.0464 (0.5)		0.0133 (0.2)	−0.0023 (0.0)	0.0383 (0.4)
$\Delta\ln p_{t-2}$		0.2087 (2.5)	0.1626 (2.0)	0.1042 (1.2)		0.1722 (2.1)	0.1509 (1.8)	0.1136 (1.3)
$\Delta\ln y_{t-1}$			0.1080 (2.7)	0.1272 (2.2)			0.0260 (0.6)	0.0316 (0.5)
$\Delta\ln y_{t-2}$			0.1029 (2.6)	0.2185 (3.8)			0.0276 (0.7)	0.1228 (2.1)
$\Delta\ln c_{t-1}$				−0.0807 (2.3)				−0.0814 (2.3)
$\Delta\ln c_{t-2}$				−0.1655 (4.7)				−0.1565 (4.5)
$\Delta\ln i_{t-1}$				0.0252 (2.2)				0.0269 (2.4)
$\Delta\ln i_{t-2}$				−0.0033 (0.3)				−0.0007 (0.6)
$\Delta\ln g_{t-1}$				−0.0068 (0.3)				−0.0029 (0.1)
$\Delta\ln g_{t-2}$				0.0130 (0.6)				0.0129 (0.6)
R^2	0.0334	0.0430	0.0731	0.1326	0.1318	0.1376	0.1441	0.2110

NOTE: Regressions are run on pooled time-series cross-sectional data, with and without fixed effects for each country; p is commodity prices, y is GDP, c is consumption, i is investment, and g is government expenditure. Numbers in parentheses are absolute t-values. The dependent variable is the growth rate of GDP ($\Delta\ln y_t$).

problematic. It is true that especially in countries where tax systems channel fluctuations in commodity-price incomes to the government, there may be political repercussions even when the rate of economic growth is unaffected.

As we shall see, it is possible to conduct some (limited) tests to see whether commodity prices work separately from their effect on national output. The models of political economy that we are considering, however, are hardly well-enough developed to draw a sharp distinction between the political effects of economic good fortune in the form of enhanced growth of the economy, or economic good fortune in the form of windfall income from commodity prices. What is of most concern is whether it is economic good fortune that determines political success or whether the reverse is true.

Table 13 corresponds to Table 9, but with the growth rate of GDP instrumented by current growth of the commodity-price index in the top panel of the table and by current and first- and second-lagged growth in the middle panel of the table. Although the second lag of commodity-price growth helps predict the growth of GDP in Table 10, the additional instruments are not guaranteed to generate more precise IV estimates, so that it is unclear which of the two top panels of Table 13 is to be preferred. Parameters are shown with and without the inclusion of the characteristics of the leaders, and as always, with and without the country fixed effects. The last two lines of the table report the Hausman-Wu test for the endogeneity of the economic growth rate; in this context, the test is a t-test for the hypothesis that the coefficient of economic growth is the same under instrumentation as when estimated by OLS methods. Also reported in the last line of the table is the overidentification F-test. When there are more instruments than endogenous variables, as is the case when the lags of price growth are included, we can compare the fit of the model as estimated with the fit of an equation in which all the exogenous variables are included without restriction. The resulting test statistic is asymptotically distributed as an F-statistic with (numerator) degrees of freedom equal to the number of exogenous variables beyond those required for identification—in this case, two.

These results are bedeviled by the same problem as beset the direct comparison of commodity prices and political exit, that is, that the two variables, although negatively correlated, are not significantly negatively correlated, so that none of the IV estimates of the effect of income growth are significantly different from zero. It should again be noted, however, that the results are exactly what would be predicted if the

TABLE 13

ECONOMIC GROWTH AND POLITICAL EXIT: INSTRUMENTAL-VARIABLE (IV) ESTIMATES

	Without Fixed Effects		With Country Fixed Effects	
Using Only Δlnp_t as Instrument				
Δlny_t	−0.3325 (0.4)	−0.4649 (0.6)	−0.4207 (0.5)	−0.2392 (0.3)
Time in power		−0.0010 (0.6)		−0.0018 (0.8)
Nonconstitutional entry		0.0694 (2.0)		−0.0569 (1.2)
Time x nonconst. entry		−0.0088 (2.2)		−0.0063 (1.4)
Hausman-Wu *t*-test	−0.23	−0.07	−0.00	−0.24
With the Addition of Once- and Twice-Lagged Δlnp_t as Instruments				
Δlny_t	−0.1725 (0.2)	−0.2954 (0.4)	−0.1589 (0.2)	0.0295 (0.0)
Time in power		−0.0009 (0.5)		0.0021 (0.9)
Nonconstitutional entry		0.0723 (2.1)		−0.0521 (1.1)
Time x nonconst. entry		−0.0087 (2.2)		−0.0061 (1.3)
Hausman-Wu *t*-test	−0.50	−0.34	−0.33	−0.62 .
Overidentification *F*-test	0.82	0.88	0.93	0.81
With the Addition of Once- and Twice-Lagged Δlnp_t, Δlny_t, Δlnc_t, and Δlng_t as Instruments				
Δlny_t	−0.7125 (1.7)	−0.6891 (1.6)	−0.4290 (0.8)	−0.4048 (0.8)
Time in power		0.0009 (0.5)		0.0038 (1.8)
Nonconstitutional entry		0.1148 (3.4)		0.0374 (0.8)
Time x nonconst. entry		−0.0126 (3.2)		−0.0079 (1.7)
Hausman-Wu *t*-test	0.79	0.74	0.18	0.15
Overidentification *F*-test	0.88	0.68	0.78	0.74

NOTE: The instrumental variables are time in power, nonconstitutional entry, and their interaction (when they are included in the main regression), together with the identifying instruments (as indicated), that is, the contemporaneous or the contemporaneous plus first and second lags of commodity-price growth measured in GDP equivalents. In the bottom panel, the instruments also include the lagged growth rates of the components of GDP shown in Table 12. Numbers in parentheses are absolute *t*-values.

baseline single-equation results were correct and thus unaffected by simultaneity bias. The IV estimates in the top two panels of Table 13, although less precise than the OLS estimates in Table 9, are essentially the same numbers. The loss in precision, moreover, is also exactly what would be predicted if the single-equation models are correct. In the simplest case, in which there is one endogenous variable and one instrument—as in the left-hand top panel of the table—the ratio of the standard error of the OLS parameter estimate to the IV parameter estimate is the correlation coefficient between the instrument and the endogenous variable, in this case, 0.18 (the square root of the R^2 statistic in the first column of Table 12). Thus, the truth of the economics-to-politics story predicts that the standard errors in Table 13 should be a little more than five times those in Table 9. This is exactly what they are. The insignificant Hausman-Wu tests give essentially the same message, that the IV estimate of the effect of economic growth on the probability of a political exit is the same as the OLS estimate. If there were important feedbacks from political exit to economic growth, we would expect the coefficient to change when these effects are removed by instrumenting economic growth with the exogenous commodity-price variable.

Of course, the evidence in favor of the economics-to-politics version of the story would be a good deal more convincing if the parameter estimates were more precise. But without further instruments, or without a stronger correlation between commodity prices and economic growth, it is not possible to do better without weakening the identifying structure. If we are prepared to do so, however, and follow the literature in assuming that earlier events are not caused by later ones, we can introduce the lagged components of GDP as instruments. Considerable attention must be paid to the overidentification tests in these experiments, because the tests are our only protection against the (quite reasonable) supposition that the lagged components of GDP growth should themselves appear as direct determinants of political exit.

The results are presented in the bottom panel of Table 13. Once again, they are not very different from the very first results in Table 9; if anything, the effects of economic growth on political exit are *larger*, which would suggest that, in the African context, any feedback from political exit is growth *enhancing*, an effect that in single-equation estimation would mute the direct negative effect of economic success on leaders' survival. The additional instruments, which have substantial predictive power for the growth of GDP, result in much more precise estimates, so that the t-values are now much closer to those for the OLS estimates in Table 9. As in the rest of the table, the Hausman-Wu tests show no evidence of endogeneity, so that the increase in the estimated coefficient is no more significant than were the decreases in the top two panels. Most important, the overidentification test statistics are insignificant, so there is no suggestion that the instruments themselves belong in the main regression. This finding is perhaps not very surprising, given the insignificance of these variables in the single-equation exit equation, but it still offers modest support for the results in the bottom panel.

Conclusions

The main conclusions have already been presented. The use of commodity prices as instrumental variables for economic growth has no effect on the robust result that economic growth inhibits political exit in Africa; there is no evidence in these data, however, to support the reverse position, that economic growth is enhanced by the absence of political exit. We make only modest claims for our results; the correlation between commodity prices and economic growth in Africa is real, but it is not sufficiently strong to allow precise inferences about parameters. Furthermore, our study has addressed only one link in the political-economic nexus, that between economic growth and political leaders' survival. Political exit is far from being the same thing as political instability, let alone democracy, and although the methods of this study can perhaps be applied to these issues, they are not addressed here. It is hard to see how questions of causality can be addressed, however, without the identification of variables that, like commodity prices, determine one set of variables, economic or political, without being affected by the other.

More substantively, it would make sense to improve the study by extending it to a larger number of countries and over a longer time period, something that is feasible at the cost of constructing the country-specific commodity-price indices. It is perhaps also possible to find other variables, perhaps measures of world production focused on individual countries, that will allow the construction of instruments that are more highly correlated with economic growth.

REFERENCES

Akiyama, Takamasa, and Ronald C. Duncan, "Analysis of the World Coffee Market," World Bank Staff Commodity Working Paper No 7, Washington, D.C., World Bank, 1982.

Alesina, Alberto, Sule Özler, Nouriel Roubini, and Philip Swagel, "Political Instability and Economic Growth," National Bureau of Economic Research Working Paper No. 4173, Cambridge, Mass., National Bureau of Economic Research, September 1992.

American Metal Market, *Metal Statistics 1978*, New York, Fairchild, 1978.

Ardeni, Pier Giorgio, and Brian Wright, "The Prebisch–Singer Hypothesis: A Reappraisal Independent of Stationarity Hypotheses," *Economic Journal*, 102 (1992), pp. 803–812.

Aron, Janine, "Mismanaged Mineral Trade Shocks: The Zambian Copper Boom and Crash (1964–80)," Oxford, Centre for the Study of African Economies, processed, February 1992.

Balassa, Bela, "Temporary Windfalls and Compensation Arrangements," World Bank Policy, Planning, and Research Working Paper Series No. 28, Washington, D.C., World Bank, 1988.

Barro, Robert J., "A Cross-Country Study of Growth, Saving, and Government," in B. Douglas Bernheim and John B. Shoven, eds., *National Saving and Economic Performance*, Chicago, Chicago University Press for National Bureau of Economic Research, 1991a, pp. 271–304.

———, "Economic Growth in a Cross-Section of Countries," *Quarterly Journal of Economics*, 106 (1991b), pp. 407–444.

Bateman, Merrill J., "Global Perspectives on Cocoa Supply and Demand," in Bateman et al., eds., "Ghana's Cocoa Pricing Policy," World Bank Policy, Planning, and Research Working Paper Series No. 429, Washington, D.C., World Bank, 1990.

Bates, Robert H., *Markets and States in Tropical Africa: The Political Basis of Agricultural Policies*, Berkeley, University of California Press, 1981.

———, "The Nature and Origins of Agricultural Policies in Africa," in Bates, *Essays on the Political Economy of Rural Africa*, Cambridge, Cambridge University Press, 1983, pp. 107–133.

———, *Beyond the Miracle of the Market: The Political Economy of Agrarian Development in Kenya*, Cambridge, Cambridge University Press, 1989.

Bauer, Peter, "Remembrance of Studies Past: Retracing First Steps," in Gerald M. Meier and Dudley Seers, eds., *Pioneers in Development*, New York, Oxford University Press for the World Bank, 1984, pp. 27–43.

Bauer, Peter, and Frank Paish, "The Reduction of Fluctuations in the Incomes of Primary Producers," *Economic Journal*, 62 (1952), pp. 750–780.

Benjamin, Dwayne, and Angus Deaton, "Household Welfare and the Pricing of Cocoa and Coffee in Côte d'Ivoire: Lessons from the Living Standards Surveys," *World Bank Economic Review*, 7 (1993), pp. 293–318.

Besley, Timothy, "Monopsony and Time-Consistency: Sustainable Pricing Policies for Perennial Crops," Princeton, N.J., Princeton University, Research Program in Development Studies Discussion Paper 159, 1992.

Bevan, David, Paul Collier, and Jan Willem Gunning, *Peasants and Governments: An Economic Analysis*, Oxford, Clarendon, 1989.

———, *Controlled Open Economies: A Neoclassical Approach to Structuralism*, Oxford, Clarendon, 1990.

———, "Temporary Trade Shocks in Developing Countries: Consequences and Policy Responses," Oxford, Centre for the Study of African Economies, processed, June 1991.

Bienen, Henry S., "Nigeria: From Windfall Gains to Welfare Losses," in Alan Gelb, *Oil Windfalls: Blessing or Curse*, New York, Oxford University Press for the World Bank, 1988, pp. 227–261.

Bienen, Henry S., John Londregan, and Nicolas van de Walle, "Ethnicity, Leadership Succession and Economic Development in Africa," Washington, D.C., Institute for Policy Reform, processed, August 1993.

Bienen, Henry S., and Nicolas van de Walle, *Of Time and Power: Leadership Duration in the Modern World*, Stanford, Calif., Stanford University Press, 1991.

———, "A Proportional Hazard Model of Leadership Duration," *Journal of Politics*, 54 (1992), pp. 685–717.

Bollen, Kenneth A., "Issues in the Comparative Measurement of Political Democracy," *American Sociological Review*, 45 (1980), pp. 370–390.

Campbell, John Y., and Pierre Perron, "Pitfalls and Opportunities: What Macroeconomists Should Know about Unit Roots," in Olivier J. Blanchard and Stanley Fischer, eds., *Macroeconomics Annual 1991*, Cambridge, Mass., MIT Press for National Bureau of Economic Research, 1991, pp. 141–201.

Cochrane, John, "How Big is the Random Walk in GDP?" *Journal of Political Economy*, 96 (1988), pp. 893–920.

———, "Comment," in Olivier J. Blanchard and Stanley Fischer, eds., *Macroeconomics Annual 1991*, Cambridge, Mass., MIT Press for National Bureau of Economic Research, 1991, pp. 201–210.

Collier, Paul, and Jan Willem Gunning, *Trade Shocks: Consequences and Policy Responses in Developing Countries*, San Francisco, International Center for Economic Growth, 1994.

———, "Trade Shocks: Theory and Experience," Chapter 1 in Paul Collier, Jan Willem Gunning, and associates, *Trade Shocks in Developing Countries*, Oxford, Oxford University Press, forthcoming 1995.

Commodity Research Bureau, *CRB Infotech Commodity Data* (CD-ROM Version 2.0), Chicago, Knight-Ridder, 1992.

Cuddington, John T., "Commodity Export Booms in Developing Countries," *World Bank Research Observer*, 4 (1989), pp. 143–165.

————, "Long-Run Trends in 26 Primary Commodity Prices: A Disaggregated Look at the Prebisch-Singer Hypothesis," *Journal of Development Economics*, 39 (1992), pp. 207-227.

Cuddington, John T., and Tarhan Feyzioglu, "Long-Run Trends in Primary Commodity Prices: Resolving Our Differences Using the ARFIMA Model," Washington, D.C., Georgetown University, processed, December 1993.

Cuddington, John T., and Carlos M. Urzúa, "Trends and Cycles in the Net Barter Terms of Trade: A New Approach," *Economic Journal*, 99 (1989), pp. 426–442.

Cukierman, Alex, Sebastian Edwards, and Guido Tabellini, "Seigniorage and Political Instability," *American Economic Review*, 82 (1992), pp. 537–555.

Dasgupta, Partha, *An Inquiry into Well-Being and Destitution*, Oxford, Clarendon, 1993.

Dasgupta, Partha, and Martin Weale, "On Measuring the Quality of Life," *World Development*, 20 (1992), pp. 119–131.

Davis, Jeffrey M., "The Economic Effects of Windfall Gains in Export Earnings 1975–78," *World Development*, 11 (1983), pp. 119–139.

Deaton, Angus, "Saving and Liquidity Constraints," *Econometrica*, 59 (1991), pp. 1221–1248.

————,"Commodity Prices, Stabilization, and Growth in Africa," Washington, D.C., Institute for Policy Reform, and Princeton, N.J., Princeton University Research Program in Development Studies, processed, April 1993a.

————, "The Price of Power: Commodity Prices and Political Survival in Africa," Washington, D.C., Institute for Policy Reform, and Princeton, N.J., Princeton University Research Program in Development Studies, processed, December 1993b.

Deaton, Angus, and Guy Laroque, "On the Behavior of Commodity Prices," *Review of Economic Studies*, 59 (1992), pp. 1–24.

————, "Competitive Storage and Commodity Price Dynamics," *Journal of Political Economy*, forthcoming 1995.

Deaton, Angus, and Ronald Miller, "Commodity Prices and Macroeconomic Management in Africa," Washington, D.C., Institute for Policy Reform, processed, November 1993.

FAO Quarterly Bulletin of Statistics, Rome, Food and Agriculture Organization of the United Nations, various years.

Friedman, Milton, "The Reduction of Fluctuations in the Incomes of Primary Producers: A Critical Comment," *Economic Journal*, 64 (1954), pp. 698–703.

Frimpong-Ansah, Jonathan H., *The Vampire State in Africa: The Political Economy of Decline in Ghana*, Trenton, N.J., Africa World Press, 1992.

Gastil, Raymond D., *Freedom in the World*, Westport, Conn., Greenwood, 1987.

Gavin, Michael, "Adjusting to a Terms of Trade Shock: Nigeria, 1972–88," in Rudiger Dornbusch, ed., *Policymaking in the Open Economy: Concepts and Case Studies in Economic Performance*, Oxford and New York, Oxford

University Press for the World Bank, 1993, pp. 172-219.

Gelb, Alan, *Oil Windfalls: Blessing or Curse*, New York, Oxford University Press for the World Bank, 1988.

Gersovitz, Mark, and Christina H. Paxson, *The Economies of Africa and the Prices of Their Exports*, Princeton Studies in International Finance No. 68, Princeton, N.J., Princeton University, International Finance Section, October 1990.

Greene, Joshua, "The External Debt Problem of Sub-Saharan Africa," *International Monetary Fund Staff Papers*, 36 (1989), pp. 836-874.

Grier, Kevin B., and Gordon Tullock, "An Empirical Analysis of Cross-National Economic Growth, 1951–80," *Journal of Monetary Economics*, 24 (1989), pp. 259–276.

Grilli, Enzo, and Maw Cheng Yang, "Primary Commodity Prices, Manufactured Goods Prices, and the Terms of Trade in Developing Countries," *World Bank Economic Review*, 2 (1988), pp. 1–47.

Helliwell, John F., "Empirical Linkages between Democracy and Economic Growth," National Bureau of Economic Research Working Paper No. 4066, Cambridge, Mass., National Bureau of Economic Research, May 1992.

Hill, Polly, *The Migrant Cocoa Farmers of Southern Ghana: A Study in Rural Capitalism*, Cambridge, Cambridge University Press, 1963.

Hirschman, Albert O., "A Generalized Linkage Approach to Development, with Special Reference to Staples," *Economic Development and Cultural Change*, 25 (Supplement, 1977), pp. 67–98.

Ingham, Barbara M., "Ghana Cocoa Farmers—Income Expenditure—Relationships," *Journal of Development Studies*, 9 (1973), pp. 365–372.

International Monetary Fund (IMF), *International Financial Statistics* (CD-ROM), Washington, D.C., International Monetary Fund, March 1994.

Killick, Tony, "Kenya, 1975–81," in Killick, ed., *The IMF and Stabilization*, London, Heinemann, 1984, pp. 164-216.

Kormendi, Roger C., and Philip G. Meguire, "Macroeconomic Determinants of Growth," *Journal of Monetary Economics*, 16 (1985), pp. 141–163.

Krueger, Anne O., "Origins of the Developing Countries' Debt Crisis, 1970 to 1982," *Journal of Development Economics*, 27 (1987), pp. 165–187.

Lewis, W. Arthur, "Economic Development with Unlimited Supplies of Labor," *Manchester School of Economics and Social Studies*, 22 (1954), pp. 139–191.

Little, Ian M.D., Richard M. Cooper, W. Max Corden, and Sarath Rajapatirana, *Boom, Crisis, and Adjustment: The Macroeconomic Experience of Developing Countries*, New York, Oxford University Press for the World Bank, 1993.

Lofchie, Michael F., *The Policy Factor: Agricultural Performance in Kenya and Tanzania*, Boulder, Colo., Lynne Rienner, 1989.

Londregan, John, and Keith T. Poole, "Poverty, the Coup Trap, and the Seizure of Executive Power," *World Politics*, 42 (1990), pp. 151–183.

Mankiw, N. Gregory, David Romer, and David Weil, "A Contribution to the Empirics of Economic Growth," *Quarterly Journal of Economics*, 107 (1992), pp. 407–437.

Mirrlees, James A., "Optimal Commodity Price Intervention," Washington, D.C., World Bank, processed, August 1988.

Newbery, David, "Implications of Imperfect Risk Markets for Agricultural Taxation," Cambridge, Cambridge University Department of Applied Economics Working Paper No. 8914, 1989.

——, "Cocoa Tax and Revenue Alternatives," in Bateman et al., eds., "Ghana's Cocoa Pricing Policy," World Bank Policy, Planning, and Research Working Paper Series No. 429, Washington, D.C., World Bank, 1990.

Özler, Sule, and Guido Tabellini, "External Debt and Political Instability," National Bureau of Economic Research Working Paper No. 3772, Cambridge, Mass., National Bureau of Economic Research, July 1991.

Paxson, Christina H., "Using Weather Variability to Estimate the Response of Savings to Transitory Income in Thailand," *American Economic Review*, 82 (1992), pp. 15–33.

——, "Consumption and Income Seasonality in Thailand," *Journal of Political Economy*, 101 (1993), pp. 39-72.

Penn World Table (Mark 5.6), Cambridge, Mass., National Bureau of Economic Research, computer file ("anonymous ftp@nber.harvard.edu").

Powell, Andrew, "Options to Alleviate the Costs of Uncertainty and Stability: A Case Study of Zambia," in Louis Phlips, ed., *Commodity, Futures and Financial Markets*, Dordecht, Kluwer, 1991, pp. 59–83.

Radetski, Marian, *Uranium: A Strategic Source of Energy*, New York, St. Martin's, 1981.

Sachs, Jeffrey D., "Introduction," in Sachs, ed., *Developing Country Debt and Economic Performance*, Vol 1., Chicago, Chicago University Press for National Bureau of Economic Research, 1988, pp. 1-35.

Scully, Gerald W., "The Institutional Framework and Economic Development," *Journal of Political Economy*, 96 (1988), pp. 652–662.

——, *Constitutional Environments and Economic Growth*, Princeton, N.J., Princeton University Press, 1992.

Sirowy, Larry, and Alex Inkeles, "The Effects of Democracy on Economic Growth and Inequality: A Review," *Studies in Comparative Economic Development*, 25 (1990), pp. 126–157.

Squire, Lyn, "Project Evaluation in Theory and Practice," in Hollis Chenery and T.N. Srinivasan, eds., *Handbook of Development Economics*, Vol. 2, Amsterdam, North-Holland, 1989, pp. 1093–1137.

Summers, Robert, and Alan Heston, "The Penn World Table (Mark 5): An Expanded Set of International Comparisons, 1950–1988," *Quarterly Journal of Economics*, 106 (1991), pp. 327–368.

Tanzi, Vito, "Fiscal Policy Responses to Exogenous Shocks," *American Economic Review*, Papers and Proceedings, 76 (1986), pp. 88–91.

United Nations (UN), *Handbook of International Trade and Development Statistics*, New York, United Nations Conference on Trade and Development, 1978.

————, *UNCTAD Commodity Yearbook*, New York, United Nations Conference on Trade and Development, various years.

————, *Yearbook of International Trade Statistics*, New York, United Nations Department of Economic and Social Affairs, 1978.

World Bank, *African Economic and Financial Data* (Version 1.0), computer diskettes, March 1990.

World Bank, *World Data* (CD-ROM), Washington, D.C., World Bank, 1994.

PUBLICATIONS OF THE
INTERNATIONAL FINANCE SECTION

Notice to Contributors

The International Finance Section publishes papers in four series: ESSAYS IN INTERNATIONAL FINANCE, PRINCETON STUDIES IN INTERNATIONAL FINANCE, and SPECIAL PAPERS IN INTERNATIONAL ECONOMICS contain new work not published elsewhere. REPRINTS IN INTERNATIONAL FINANCE reproduce journal articles previously published by Princeton faculty members associated with the Section. The Section welcomes the submission of manuscripts for publication under the following guidelines:

ESSAYS are meant to disseminate new views about international financial matters and should be accessible to well-informed nonspecialists as well as to professional economists. Technical terms, tables, and charts should be used sparingly; mathematics should be avoided.

STUDIES are devoted to new research on international finance, with preference given to empirical work. They should be comparable in originality and technical proficiency to papers published in leading economic journals. They should be of medium length, longer than a journal article but shorter than a book.

SPECIAL PAPERS are surveys of research on particular topics and should be suitable for use in undergraduate courses. They may be concerned with international trade as well as international finance. They should also be of medium length.

Manuscripts should be submitted in triplicate, typed single sided and double spaced throughout on 8½ by 11 white bond paper. Publication can be expedited if manuscripts are computer keyboarded in WordPerfect 5.1 or a compatible program. Additional instructions and a style guide are available from the Section.

How to Obtain Publications

The Section's publications are distributed free of charge to college, university, and public libraries and to nongovernmental, nonprofit research institutions. Eligible institutions may ask to be placed on the Section's permanent mailing list.

Individuals and institutions not qualifying for free distribution may receive all publications for the calendar year for a subscription fee of $40.00. Late subscribers will receive all back issues for the year during which they subscribe. Subscribers should notify the Section promptly of any change in address, giving the old address as well as the new.

Publications may be ordered individually, with payment made in advance. ESSAYS and REPRINTS cost $8.00 each; STUDIES and SPECIAL PAPERS cost $11.00. An additional $1.50 should be sent for postage and handling within the United States, Canada, and Mexico; $1.75 should be added for surface delivery outside the region.

All payments must be made in U.S. dollars. Subscription fees and charges for single issues will be waived for organizations and individuals in countries where foreign-exchange regulations prohibit dollar payments.

Please address all correspondence, submissions, and orders to:

International Finance Section
Department of Economics, Fisher Hall
Princeton University
Princeton, New Jersey 08544-1021

List of Recent Publications

A complete list of publications may be obtained from the International Finance Section.

ESSAYS IN INTERNATIONAL FINANCE

162. Stephen E. Haynes, Michael M. Hutchison, and Raymond F. Mikesell, *Japanese Financial Policies and the U.S. Trade Deficit.* (April 1986)
163. Arminio Fraga, *German Reparations and Brazilian Debt: A Comparative Study.* (July 1986)
164. Jack M. Guttentag and Richard J. Herring, *Disaster Myopia in International Banking.* (September 1986)
165. Rudiger Dornbusch, *Inflation, Exchange Rates, and Stabilization.* (October 1986)
166. John Spraos, *IMF Conditionality: Ineffectual, Inefficient, Mistargeted.* (December 1986)
167. Rainer Stefano Masera, *An Increasing Role for the ECU: A Character in Search of a Script.* (June 1987)
168. Paul Mosley, *Conditionality as Bargaining Process: Structural-Adjustment Lending, 1980-86.* (October 1987)
169. Paul A. Volcker, Ralph C. Bryant, Leonhard Gleske, Gottfried Haberler, Alexandre Lamfalussy, Shijuro Ogata, Jesús Silva-Herzog, Ross M. Starr, James Tobin, and Robert Triffin, *International Monetary Cooperation: Essays in Honor of Henry C. Wallich.* (December 1987)
170. Shafiqul Islam, *The Dollar and the Policy-Performance-Confidence Mix.* (July 1988)
171. James M. Boughton, *The Monetary Approach to Exchange Rates: What Now Remains?* (October 1988)
172. Jack M. Guttentag and Richard M. Herring, *Accounting for Losses On Sovereign Debt: Implications for New Lending.* (May 1989)
173. Benjamin J. Cohen, *Developing-Country Debt: A Middle Way.* (May 1989)
174. Jeffrey D. Sachs, *New Approaches to the Latin American Debt Crisis.* (July 1989)
175. C. David Finch, *The IMF: The Record and the Prospect.* (September 1989)
176. Graham Bird, *Loan-Loss Provisions and Third-World Debt.* (November 1989)
177. Ronald Findlay, *The "Triangular Trade" and the Atlantic Economy of the Eighteenth Century: A Simple General-Equilibrium Model.* (March 1990)
178. Alberto Giovannini, *The Transition to European Monetary Union.* (November 1990)
179. Michael L. Mussa, *Exchange Rates in Theory and in Reality.* (December 1990)
180. Warren L. Coats, Jr., Reinhard W. Furstenberg, and Peter Isard, *The SDR System and the Issue of Resource Transfers.* (December 1990)
181. George S. Tavlas, *On the International Use of Currencies: The Case of the Deutsche Mark.* (March 1991)
182. Tommaso Padoa-Schioppa, ed., with Michael Emerson, Kumiharu Shigehara, and Richard Portes, *Europe After 1992: Three Essays.* (May 1991)

183. Michael Bruno, *High Inflation and the Nominal Anchors of an Open Economy.* (June 1991)

184. Jacques J. Polak, *The Changing Nature of IMF Conditionality.* (September 1991)

185. Ethan B. Kapstein, *Supervising International Banks: Origins and Implications of the Basle Accord.* (December 1991)

186. Alessandro Giustiniani, Francesco Papadia, and Daniela Porciani, *Growth and Catch-Up in Central and Eastern Europe: Macroeconomic Effects on Western Countries.* (April 1992)

187. Michele Fratianni, Jürgen von Hagen, and Christopher Waller, *The Maastricht Way to EMU.* (June 1992)

188. Pierre-Richard Agénor, *Parallel Currency Markets in Developing Countries: Theory, Evidence, and Policy Implications.* (November 1992)

189. Beatriz Armendariz de Aghion and John Williamson, *The G-7's Joint-and-Several Blunder.* (April 1993)

190. Paul Krugman, *What Do We Need to Know About the International Monetary System?* (July 1993)

191. Peter M. Garber and Michael G. Spencer, *The Dissolution of the Austro-Hungarian Empire: Lessons for Currency Reform.* (February 1994)

192. Raymond F. Mikesell, *The Bretton Woods Debates: A Memoir.* (March 1994)

193. Graham Bird, *Economic Assistance to Low-Income Countries: Should the Link be Resurrected?* (July 1994)

194. Lorenzo Bini-Smaghi, Tommaso Padoa-Schioppa, and Francesco Papadia, *The Transition to EMU in the Maastricht Treaty.* (November 1994)

195. Ariel Buira, *Reflections on the International Monetary System.* (January 1995)

196. Shinji Takagi, *From Recipient to Donor: Japan's Official Aid Flows, 1945 to 1990 and Beyond.* (March 1995)

197. Patrick Conway, *Currency Proliferation: The Monetary Legacy of the Soviet Union.* (June 1995)

PRINCETON STUDIES IN INTERNATIONAL FINANCE

57. Stephen S. Golub, *The Current-Account Balance and the Dollar: 1977-78 and 1983-84.* (October 1986)

58. John T. Cuddington, *Capital Flight: Estimates, Issues, and Explanations.* (December 1986)

59. Vincent P. Crawford, *International Lending, Long-Term Credit Relationships, and Dynamic Contract Theory.* (March 1987)

60. Thorvaldur Gylfason, *Credit Policy and Economic Activity in Developing Countries with IMF Stabilization Programs.* (August 1987)

61. Stephen A. Schuker, *American "Reparations" to Germany, 1919-33: Implications for the Third-World Debt Crisis.* (July 1988)

62. Steven B. Kamin, *Devaluation, External Balance, and Macroeconomic Performance: A Look at the Numbers.* (August 1988)

63. Jacob A. Frenkel and Assaf Razin, *Spending, Taxes, and Deficits: International-Intertemporal Approach.* (December 1988)

64. Jeffrey A. Frankel, *Obstacles to International Macroeconomic Policy Coordination.* (December 1988)

65. Peter Hooper and Catherine L. Mann, *The Emergence and Persistence of the U.S. External Imbalance, 1980-87.* (October 1989)
66. Helmut Reisen, *Public Debt, External Competitiveness, and Fiscal Discipline in Developing Countries.* (November 1989)
67. Victor Argy, Warwick McKibbin, and Eric Siegloff, *Exchange-Rate Regimes for a Small Economy in a Multi-Country World.* (December 1989)
68. Mark Gersovitz and Christina H. Paxson, *The Economies of Africa and the Prices of Their Exports.* (October 1990)
69. Felipe Larraín and Andrés Velasco, *Can Swaps Solve the Debt Crisis? Lessons from the Chilean Experience.* (November 1990)
70. Kaushik Basu, *The International Debt Problem, Credit Rationing and Loan Pushing: Theory and Experience.* (October 1991)
71. Daniel Gros and Alfred Steinherr, *Economic Reform in the Soviet Union: Pas de Deux between Disintegration and Macroeconomic Destabilization.* (November 1991)
72. George M. von Furstenberg and Joseph P. Daniels, *Economic Summit Declarations, 1975-1989: Examining the Written Record of International Cooperation.* (February 1992)
73. Ishac Diwan and Dani Rodrik, *External Debt, Adjustment, and Burden Sharing: A Unified Framework.* (November 1992)
74. Barry Eichengreen, *Should the Maastricht Treaty Be Saved?* (December 1992)
75. Adam Klug, *The German Buybacks, 1932-1939: A Cure for Overhang?* (November 1993)
76. Tamim Bayoumi and Barry Eichengreen, *One Money or Many? Analyzing the Prospects for Monetary Unification in Various Parts of the World.* (September 1994)
77. Edward E. Leamer, *The Heckscher-Ohlin Model in Theory and Practice.* (February 1995)
78. Thorvaldur Gylfason, *The Macroeconomics of European Agriculture.* (May 1995)
79. Angus S. Deaton and Ronald I. Miller, *International Commodity Prices, Macroeconomic Performance, and Politics in Sub-Saharan Africa.* (December 1995)

SPECIAL PAPERS IN INTERNATIONAL ECONOMICS

16. Elhanan Helpman, *Monopolistic Competition in Trade Theory.* (June 1990)
17. Richard Pomfret, *International Trade Policy with Imperfect Competition.* (August 1992)
18. Hali J. Edison, *The Effectiveness of Central-Bank Intervention: A Survey of the Literature After 1982.* (July 1993)

REPRINTS IN INTERNATIONAL FINANCE

27. Peter B. Kenen, *Transitional Arrangements for Trade and Payments Among the CMEA Countries*; reprinted from *International Monetary Fund Staff Papers* 38 (2), 1991. (July 1991)
28. Peter B. Kenen, *Ways to Reform Exchange-Rate Arrangements*; reprinted from *Bretton Woods: Looking to the Future*, 1994. (November 1994)